Preparing for Your Prime Time

A Woman Boomer's Guide To Retirement

Preparing for Your Prime Time

A Woman Boomer's Guide To Retirement

Molly Dickinson Shepard
with
Susannah Cobb & Starla Crandall

Copyedited and indexed by April Joyce MdR Aquino
Reviewed by Jill Marie Duero

This book was printed in the United States of America.

To order additional copies of this book, contact:
Xlibris Corporation
1-888-795-4274
www.Xlibris.com
Orders@Xlibris.com
111602

I wish to dedicate this book to my granddaughters Kaia and Devon who will be reaching their retirements six decades from now. May you both arrive there safely and enjoy your retirement years!

TABLE OF CONTENTS

ACKNOWLEDGMENTS

I would like to thank Ellie Thompson for her encouragement to write this book and for allowing me to go along with her on her journey to a retirement career. Also, my deepest thanks and gratitude to Jane Stimmler who does more than just edit brilliantly. Her advice and direction are always appreciated. I also wish to thank Susannah Cobb and Starla Crandall for their invaluable assistance in writing this important book. And a special acknowledgment to all my friends who, like me, are of a "certain age" and may take some tips from this book as they venture with me into the unknown.

Women. They are a complete mystery.
—Stephen Hawking

PROLOGUE

A Big Black Hole

Joan was one of those people who really loved her job. She had an important position with a pharmaceutical company, and though she put in long hours, she felt valued by her colleagues and enjoyed her work. She was well aware that most Americans go to work each day feeling unhappy, and she was grateful that she wasn't one of them. At age sixty, she felt she was lucky to be in such a great place. So when Joan learned about the new early retirement program her company was offering, she paid little attention until she realized that the benefits, if she chose to retire, were too generous to ignore. Joan had mixed feelings about this important decision. She knew that she was young enough to work for another five to ten years. Her parents were in their late eighties, so if she followed suit, she would need enough income to provide her with a full and independent life for many years to come. Most difficult for her was what she would do in retirement since her job played such a major role in her life—both from a business standpoint and through her many work friends. Since she hadn't thought much about retirement, she realized she had very little information and a lot of questions. In fact, it felt like she was looking into a big black hole. The rules didn't allow her to speak to anyone in the company about her decision, so she sought my help to sort through all the factors. It is Joan's and all the other women's journeys to whom this book is dedicated.

Prime Time redefines the rules of work—and life—for women thinking about the next phase of their lives: retirement. This book helps you prepare for the rest of your life, instead of letting it happen *to* you. If you are stuck in a rut, out of a job, sick and tired of what you've been doing, or yearning to try something new—*Prime Time* will help you explore the big question, *what's next?*

Prime Time provides a road map for women who are ready to prepare for one of the most interesting journeys of all, the journey from the traditional workforce and into a new life of fun, freedom, and fulfillment. Typically, when you don't have a plan, retirement can look pretty scary. Once you begin to think it through, things will become much clearer. Women are resourceful and highly adaptive to change. I have seen this time and time again in more than thirty years of consulting to professional women who have grappled with serious life and career decisions after they lost their jobs, elected to change careers, professions, and lifestyles, or moved upward into more demanding and strategic leadership roles. With women's excellent relationship-building skills, their naturally analytic thought processes, and their courage to take significant personal risks, they are well suited to engage in the exploration, analysis, and resolution needed for the retirement decision-making process.

Prime Time is your gateway to a private space in which you can explore your dreams, plan for your future, take a good look at yourself, and follow a decision-making process that leads to personal and professional happiness. We'll look at financial issues, helping you analyze what you can afford and/or need to earn to finance your plan. And not only will this book guide you through strategies and tips that will make the retirement decision-making process interesting and fun, you will hear the stories of many women who have taken the leap and are happier for doing so.

Imagine a guidebook to help you explore your dreams and possibilities; plan for personal and professional enjoyment; address any feelings of inadequacy and irrelevance; and then take you through a decision-making process that leads to fulfillment, gratification, and happiness.

We will approach your prime time in a fun but serious manner as befits its importance, helping you change course and find a new direction—one you can embark upon with knowledge, wisdom, and experience. Let us take you on the most exhilarating ride of your life as we help you look at options based on your individual strengths, accomplishments, and interests.

What do *you* want to do with the rest of your life?

A Big Black Hole No Longer

Joan and I talked in depth about the skills and abilities that she used when she was most satisfied in her work. We determined that those were the areas of expertise she could draw on if she chose to leave her company. Feeling more confident and self-assured, she scheduled meetings with professional women who had retired early and moved on to other careers. She wanted to understand how successful they were in their new endeavors and what strategies and tools they used. In addition, she spoke with colleagues and friends to get their views about the next phase of her life. She combined all this information with the results of a financial planning exercise and was then able to craft a retirement strategy that worked for her. She realized that she could not turn down the lucrative retirement package offered by her company, so she took the plunge and accepted the deal. Joan is now busy teaching part time at a major university, consulting, volunteering, helping her ailing mother, reading, fixing up her home, and lunching with old friends. She smiled when she told me she doesn't know how she ever got anything done while she was working in her old job.

All you need is a plan, a roadmap, and the courage to press on to your destination.
—E. Nightingale

CHAPTER 1

Developing Your Road Map— Making the Next Years the Best

Every day for the next eighteen years, an estimated five thousand women in the United States will turn 65, according to the Pew Research Center. Baby boomer women have been working, planning, and saving for decades to reach this moment in their lives—retirement. While it may seem daunting, it can be one of the most exciting times in your life. Think of it as a blank canvas; it is there for you to fill in as you want. Your retirement is the opportunity for you to live in your prime!

But are you prepared?

Unfortunately, the majority of women who reach 65 are not prepared for the next stage of their lives. You've taken a great first step by reading this book; however, first, let's talk about what retirement actually means in today's world. Certainly it means different things to different people and can happen at almost any age from 50 to 80. The years when everyone—mostly men—got their gold watches and ceremoniously left the working world at 65, are over. These days,

As women approach the end of their traditional workforce roles, the desire to "give back" often becomes stronger. At the same time, many women notice their insecurities begin to fade and they no longer obsess about what people think. The freedom that this gives a woman is close to magical.

not only do people work longer, but many want to continue being active even after they leave what they are doing. Thirty-five percent of the leading edge boomers (those 61 or older) have explored possible employment in retirement, according to MetLife Mature Market Institute. So a number of retirement-age people don't really retire at all—they just change course.

There are many factors that drive decisions about retirement, including finances, family obligations, personality type, and health. Some people have saved enough to retire completely from the traditional workforce without significantly altering their lifestyles. Many others want or need to continue work, hopefully doing something new and more personally rewarding. My friend Colleen, who started and runs her own company, views work as part of her identity. She often says, "I will die working at my desk. I love what I do and have no intention of retiring." For others, retirement will be dictated by health issues or a need to lessen stress. Which scenarios best describe you?

Quiz: When you think about retiring, is it because . . .
- You are tired?
- You are feeling more stress?
- Work is taking a toll on your health?
- You want to spend more time with your friends and family?
- Your spouse or partner has recently retired?
- You want to devote more time to a hobby or cause?
- Your company has a lucrative retirement package?
- You'd like to relocate to a warmer or different climate?
- You are bored with your job?
- You want to do something incredibly different with your life?

The fact is that finances will play a large role in retirement planning. A majority of people are likely to need to work to supplement insufficient retirement funds. The *Wall Street Journal* estimates that someone age 60 to 62 right now, with exactly a median level of 401(k) savings, for example, will have a 40 percent funding gap between what they will need to live (at an 85 percent replacement of their salary) and what they will receive from 401(k) retirement income and social security.

If you are now seriously thinking about retirement and contemplating various scenarios for yourself, you also may have observed firsthand that the ten years prior to the traditional retirement age can be an awfully busy decade. Now, finally, you are a professional in your prime. You have earned that fancy title, and you log long hours to complete demanding work and maintain your edge. You may also be a primary caretaker, tending to the needs of elderly parents while also continuing to financially and emotionally support your teenage or adult children. If your children are out of the house, you might find yourself taking care of grandchildren on the weekends. In fact, research from Prudential Financial indicates that six of ten retirees are caring for someone in the period five years before or after retirement—and of course, these care duties tend to fall disproportionately to women.

Maggie is still several years away from retirement and fully engaged as an entrepreneur—working happily and diligently as a principal at her consulting firm. Her parents, at age ninety-one and ninety-two, are becoming increasingly frail and needy in terms of time and attention. Maggie also has three adult children in various stages of their careers, and they frequently need her time and support. Her oldest daughter recently had twins, and Maggie tries to step in as much as she can to give her daughter a break. Maggie is where many women find themselves, caught in the traditional "sandwich"—the squeeze between elderly parents, children, and now grandchildren. And while Maggie derives an enormous amount of pleasure from most of these activities, they can be exhausting. Maggie has come to realize that her story is not so different from many other women. She knows too that she needs to give some real thought to her retirement and what will become of her business. Will she make the time now to think her retirement through?

Here's the catch about retirement: it requires your time, energy, and attention while your career and personal life are in full swing. Planning for your prime time is not as complicated as you might think, however. Keep reading, and this book will help you take a look at your life to date—the choices you've made, good and bad—and will show you how to use that information to shape a retirement plan that will allow you to do the things that inspire you, fulfill you, and meet your needs.

Given our natural tendencies, we women can have a lot of fun with the retirement planning process. Women, because of the way our brains are configured, tend to move very easily between the left side and the right side of the brain when approaching almost any problem, often employing both a creative and a practical point of view. Simply stated, women can use their right and left brain simultaneously when addressing a task or solving a problem. As a result, women often see a problem and its solution from multiple perspectives. Women can combine the desire to create a retirement scenario that draws upon their most heartfelt dreams and aspirations yet still be practical and realistic about money.

Elaine and Bill were always too busy to talk about retirement—they had their hands full, growing their family and successfully making it through each phase of their lives. Married for thirty-five years, they thought they knew everything about each other. One night, when they finally took the time to sit down and discuss the subject of retirement, they were surprised at what they learned. They had both made assumptions about where they would live and what they would do in retirement. As they talked it through though, they realized there were several attractive alternatives they had never considered. A door was opened that would ultimately change the shape of their retirement planning.

Let's not forget that in retirement planning, there is usually, although not always, a partner or spouse in the picture. Bringing your partner into this process might give you some additional insights and result in a plan that works well for both of you. The subject is, for that conversation, "What does retirement look like to me?" We highly recommend that you choose a good time for both of you, select an excellent bottle of wine, sit down, and share your answers to the following questions.

- ❖ How happy are you with what you are currently doing?
- ❖ What have you done that was most satisfying?
- ❖ How long do you see yourself working?
- ❖ What do you dream about doing in your retirement?
- ❖ What part of that fantasy includes me?
- ❖ Would you really want to have breakfast, lunch, and dinner with me every day?
- ❖ Are there any activities or hobbies that you want to take up? Do you see me involved?
- ❖ Would you want to move, and if so, where, when, and why?
- ❖ What could get in our way of personal togetherness and happiness?
- ❖ Are you excited about the future?

The answers to these questions, and the discussions they inspire, may be a little tough because you and your partner may have differing expectations. Perhaps you have fears and uncertainties. Most women do. If you are used to being apart during the day in different environments, it may be hard to imagine spending more time together. That is all okay. If there are concerns, talk about them. By the time the wine is finished, you may have had the best and most open discussion in years.

What did you find out from your conversation, and what does it mean? Has the discussion led you in any direction? Has it confirmed some of your thoughts and ideas? Before you go too far, however, there's some housekeeping to be done. You'll need to realistically understand what your finances are and how they will impact your decision making.

Let's Get to Money!

You don't need us to tell you that the financial aspect of retirement is always a primary concern and often a major determinant in what the future will look like. It all seems to come down to the eternal question, *how much money do I need for retirement?*

A survey of career baby boomers earning $75,000-plus per year shows that 62 percent of professional women fear they may never have enough to retire (MetLife Mature Market Institute, 2010). Moreover, 65 percent of women report that they feel behind schedule in savings (Prudential). Since women will live five years longer than men in retirement, on average, you need to take steps now to shore up your financial health! Identifying all your financial resources and making decisions about your current investments, including 401(k) contribution amounts and allocations, Roth IRAs, personal investments, and other expected income sources, will help you set realistic expectations as you make tangible life plans now.

We recommend you try one of the many online retirement savings calculators to estimate your total savings. Many financial institutions, including Vanguard, Fidelity, or Bankrate, have built fairly sophisticated and intuitive tools to help you. In the meantime, here's a worksheet to get you thinking about what your income and expenses are likely to look like in retirement:

Your Retirement Income and Expense Worksheet

ASSETS

1a. Calculate your total household savings expected at retirement.

Total value of 401(k), IRA, 403(b), 457, or other tax-advantaged savings plans	
Total value of other investments and investment properties	
Cash value of life insurance	
Cash accounts (checking, savings, money market)	
Savings bonds	
Home and land equity	
Other: _____	
Other: _____	
Total	$

1b. Choose a possible monthly household income range based on the total household retirement savings from question 1a:*

More than $2 million	$6,667+
$1.5 million–$2 million	$5,000–$6,667
$1 million–$1.5	$3,333–$5,000
$750,000–$1 million	$2,500–$3,333
$500,000–$750,000	$1,667–$2,500
$250,000–$500,000	$833–$1,667
$100,000–$250,000	$333–$833
Less than $100,000	0–$333
Estimate of monthly income from savings*	$

2. Calculate other sources of your household's (you and your spouse's) predetermined *monthly* income in retirement.

Social security	
Pension	
Annuities	
Other: _____	
Other: _____	
Total	$

3. Add your total household estimated monthly income (add total from question 1b and 2).

Possible monthly return, based on assets (question 1b)	
Monthly income, based on other predetermined sources (question 2)	
Total monthly income	$

EXPENSES

4. Estimate your expenses in retirement on a monthly basis (remember that most expenses will be higher in the future).

Housing (mortgage, rent, taxes, insurance)	
Home repairs	
Transportation (car loans, insurance, fuel, upkeep, travel expenses)	
Personal debt	
Insurance (health, dental, umbrella, life, other)	
Medical care and prescriptions	
Education/tuition	
Entertainment/travel	
Utilities	
Other: _____	
Other: _____	
Total known expenses	$

5. Subtract your estimated monthly expense from monthly income in retirement.

Total income (question 3)	
Total expense (question 4)	
Net income/expense in retirement	$

*All estimates are in 2011 dollars and do not consider inflation. Use this worksheet for illustrative purposes only, and seek professional advice as needed (Vanguard).

**Assumes 6 percent market returns after retirement (moderate return rate) and an average life expectancy at 65 years old, with 3 percent inflation (historical average) and a 4 percent annual withdrawal. All estimates are in 2011 dollars. Assumptions were built by the author using Vanguard's Retirement Strategies Tool: https://retirementplans.vanguard.com/VGApp/pe/pubeducation/calculators/RetirementIncomeCalc.jsf?cbdForceDomain=true

As a reminder, the previous worksheet is simply a starting place to begin to think about how much money you will need in retirement, and it is not meant to take the place of professional guidance.

There are various elements of life that can't be calculated using a worksheet or calculator. Although unpredictable and quite varied, it is important to think about some of the risks or inevitable life surprises for which you will want to build a cushion in your retirement plan. Some questions you might want to ask yourself include the following:

- Will I need/want to help my children, grandchildren, or parents financially?
- Should I allocate money for long-term care in case I am unable to care for myself?
- How expensive are my desired hobbies or activities?
- Do I need to have extra funds in case I live longer than expected?
- If I want to move, are the expenses lower or higher in the new location?
- Are there other expenses or risks that I can anticipate or plan ahead for?

Depending on your answers to these questions, here are some *prime points* to consider.

Prime Point 1: What do I need to change—if anything—about my financial situation to ensure I have saved enough?

Lucy is a fifty-five-year-old scientist who works for a biotechnology firm. She has about $175,000 in her 401(k) and personal investments of $80,000. With her husband's 401(k) and the addition of a likely inheritance from her mother when she dies, she estimates that she and her husband will have a total of $800,000 or more by the time they retire in ten years.

When calculating your income and expenses for retirement, don't forget a very important category—travel and entertainment!

Lucy always imagined that nearly $1 million in retirement savings would be enough. But she and her husband want to live comfortably, travel, and feel secure

that their savings are going to last. Her best friend just purchased a second home on Costa Rica's Pacific coast and keeps on telling her that once they all retire, they should just plan to spend the winter months there. But after Lucy estimates her and her husband's likely income in retirement, she realizes they will be 30–40 percent short of what they need. Lucy is disheartened. After being so vigilant in saving, she is shocked that they won't have enough money for their retirement dream.

Over dinner one evening, Lucy and her husband have a frank conversation and decide they must save more. They first look to maximize tax-advantaged savings. By cutting back on entertainment and dinners at restaurants, Lucy knows she can easily increase her 401(k) monthly savings, adding about $125 per paycheck and $3,000 additional per year. It's really not much compared to helping to pay for their daughter's last year of graduate school, but it will boost Lucy's personal cumulative retirement savings about $50,000 in less than ten years (assuming 6 percent annual returns and a 50 percent employee match on the first 6 percent of savings). Lucy also can make an additional $5,500 annual 401(k) "catch up" contribution, which she decides to fund with her annual bonus.

Baby boomers are turning 65 at a rate of 10,000 per day and are fully expected to enjoy an additional 20–30 years of healthy, productive living. Fifty years ago, the average life span of someone retiring was less than 70 years of age, compared to 80.1 years today.

But 3 percent more a month, with a "catch up" contribution, is not going to get Lucy and her husband to true retirement income security, so Lucy's husband also increases his monthly 401(k) contribution. Lucy has a personal IRA and joint brokerage accounts with her husband, and they recommit to maximizing their annual IRA contribution. Beginning next year, both pledge to put what they have paid for their daughter's graduate school straight into savings. With these changes, Lucy feels that they have a better chance of reaching the amount they need for the retirement they have imagined.

Lucy illustrates some of the best news about retirement planning: it's never too late to take action to improve your financial outcomes. And according to an AP-LifeGoesStrong.com poll, about 1 in 10 baby boomers in 2011 said they have saved at least $500,000. The other good news is that most women can afford to save a little bit more. According to a 2011 ING study, nearly

90 percent of workers reported they could increase their annual retirement savings contribution rate by 1 percent, and 59 percent said they could increase their contribution by 3 percent.

There's some not-so-good news too. Regardless of how diligently baby boomers have saved, most have not saved nearly enough. In 2010, the Employee Benefit Research Institute projected that 47 percent of the leading edge of baby boomers (individuals born from 1948 to 1954) are at risk in retirement of not having sufficient income to pay for even basic living expenditures and health care costs not covered by Medicare. Even among individuals in the top one-third of income, retirement savings are inadequate. The EBRI projection model also found that about 45 percent of younger boomers were also at risk of being unable to pay minimum expenses.

Half of all Americans age 50 to 70 are seeking meaningful activities during their retirement years. Good financial planning is the basis of meaningful retirement.

Hopefully, you are not in the group that will be unable to meet minimum living expenses in retirement. As a professional, you may have been able to save more across a lifetime. But many of us

do fall short of the exemplar savings and discipline of Lucy in the previous story. So what do you do if you are between these two extremes?

Below is a checklist with nine actions that you can take immediately and will make an impact in helping you save more. My experience is that, when asked, almost no one is taking even two-thirds of the actions listed below. How many of these are you doing now? And our challenge is, how many positive changes can you make immediately?

Nine Strategies for Saving More and Spending Less

1. Have you paid off credit card debt?

The average American is carrying about $9,000 in credit card debt and paying 15 percent or more on that amount (Suze Orman). Moreover, nearly 65 percent of preretirees have credit card debt according to Vanguard (2009).

Action Item: Pay down—and then *put* down—your credit cards. If you have more than one, Suze Orman recommends that you pay down the one that is charging you the highest interest while making minimum payments on the others. Going forward, don't use credit cards that you can't bring down to a zero balance immediately.

2. Are you contributing to your workplace defined contribution (DC) plan at a level that takes full advantage of any contribution match that your employer may offer?

Seventy-seven percent of plans managed by Vanguard offer 50 cents on the dollar on the first 6 percent of pay, but 55 percent of employees contributing to a DC plan save less than 6 percent (Vanguard, How America Saves, 2011).

Action Item: Check your company's employee handbook to determine the retirement plan match that is offered, and make sure that your contribution is at or above the level needed to optimize the match.

Compare your company's retirement plan benefits to others at www.brightscope.com. BrightScope scores the retirement plans of forty-five thousand companies. If you are considering moving to a new firm, make sure that you know what retirement benefits the company offers.

3. Are you contributing the maximum value to your DC plan and to your IRA?

The current annual contribution limit is $16,500 total for a DC ($22,000 over age 50), and $5,000 total for IRAs. During 2010, only 9 percent of participants saved the maximum dollar amount (Vanguard, How America Saves, 2011).

Action Item: Immediately increase retirement savings by 2–3 percent if you can. Consider the most recent industry guidance that total plan contributions (inclusive of your employer's match) should equal about 12–15 percent of your salary.

4. Are you making "catch up" contributions to your workplace savings plan and IRA?

The average household aged 60 to 62 with a 401(k) account has less than a quarter of what is needed in retirement to maintain a standard of living (the Wall Street Journal, citing the Center for Retirement Research at Boston College). Moreover, only 15 percent of US households contributed to any type of IRA in tax year 2009, according to the Investment Company Institute.

Action Item: Make annual "catch up" contributions beginning the year you turn fifty, if you can afford it. Pledge to earmark some (or all) of any annual bonus to catch up retirement contributions.

5. Are you paying on a mortgage? If so, are you making any effort to pay down the principal?

Nearly half of retirees have a mortgage (Vanguard, 2009).

Action Item: Pay a little extra toward the principal of your house every month, or consider refinancing to a fifteen-year mortgage rather than a traditional thirty-year mortgage.

6. If you have owned a home for several years, do you know whether or not it is advantageous to refinance the mortgage at a lower rate?

Nearly 40 percent of homeowners in 2011 are still paying 6 percent or more in interest on their mortgages while only 16 percent enjoy 4–5 percent fixed rate according to JP Morgan. With thirty-year mortgage rates so low, refinancing can significantly reduce your monthly payments.

Action Item: Refinance when interest rates are 2 percent lower than your current rate as an industry rule of thumb. Do your homework before you commit, however, using online mortgage calculators available at Mortgage101.com or Bankrate.com, to determine if you can get a lower monthly payment or shorter mortgage payoff period. Get mortgage estimates from multiple lenders, and be sure to consider closing costs in your decision to refinance.

7. Do you have the right investment mix for your age?

More than 60 percent of employees in DC plans are either invested too aggressively or conservatively for their age (Fidelity Investments, 2011).

Action Item: If you have an advisor, ask him or her to make sure your investments are appropriate for your age, income, and risk appetite. Consider moving your DC plan savings to a fund built around your retirement date if you are unsure of how much investment risk you should be taking. A target retirement date fund will have an appropriate risk profile and investment strategy for your age group. And make sure that the expenses on the fund are competitive.

8. Do you know how much you pay in fund management and expense fees both in your personal and workplace investments?

Sixty-two percent of participants are unaware of the fees they are paying for their 401(k) plans, according to AARP. Warren Buffett memorably cautioned Berkshire Hathaway shareholders a few years ago that "excitement and expenses are their enemies" (Allianz, *Behavioral Finance and the Post-Retirement Crisis*, 2011). *This holds even truer today.*

Action Item: Ask your financial advisor, if you work with one, to help you understand the real dollar impact of costs. Your fees are typically listed in percentage terms, not concrete dollars, making it hard to calculate your true cost. And by all means, make cost a key consideration as you review your workplace retirement plan options. Given the recent turmoil of global markets, perhaps the only element of return you can manage is cost.

9. Are you contributing to a 529 if you know you will be paying for a child or grandchild's education in the future?

The average 529 account balance is $9,700 (March 2009), while the College Board estimates that the average cost of tuition and fees for the 2011–2012 school year was $28,500 at private colleges (CollegeData.com).

Action Item: Maximize 529 contributions after you have reached the cap on your DC workplace and IRA plans. The annual contribution cap for an individual is $11,000 ($22,000 for a couple) after which you may incur taxes associated with making a gift.

We have talked about saving more and spending less. But perhaps the most critical action you can take to improve your retirement outlook is continuing to work. While 49 percent of workers age 55 and above said they would need $250,000 or more in savings and investments for retirement, only 23 percent of that same group reported savings and investments that exceeded that level, not including house or DC plan values (EBRI, Retirement Confidence Survey, *Age Comparisons Among Workers,* 2010). So it's important to approach your retirement the same way you've approached each career move—plan carefully, know your interests, analyze your strengths, and use your network to gain fresh ideas and design a plan with plenty of time to explore.

Prime Point 2: If I do work in retirement, what do I want to do and how much time will I spend doing it?

When Carrie retired at age sixty from her executive position, Carrie knew that she and her husband had plenty of financial resources. Though money wasn't a concern, one of her retirement goals was to find a board of directors position at a nonprofit organization where she could feel good about contributing her skills and experience. On the other hand, Ella,

According to Hewitt Associates, the average for-profit board of directors' salary is $67,262/year. However the salaries vary greatly due to company, location, industry, experience, and benefits.

who at age sixty-three determined that she needed to boost her retirement income, determined that she would showcase her background and accomplishments to find a board position at a for-profit company where she could make enough of a salary to allow her to travel, take cooking classes, and have the little extras. While Carrie would naturally have multiple opportunities to serve on a nonprofit board, Ella faced a daunting challenge given the statistics for women on for-profit boards. In fact, only about 16 percent of board positions at Fortune 500 companies were held by women in 2011. However, Ella wanted the opportunity enough to give it a try.

Baby boomers remain an optimistic bunch. The AARP found that most middle-aged individuals believe their lives will be better in five years than it is now. The most optimistic of this group is boomer women: 67 percent say they expect a high quality of life in five years (AARP, 2010).

How women spend leisure time will deeply impact the quality of retirement. Without forethought and planning, retirement reality can fall significantly short of what we imagine. Early retirees spend 50 percent more time in retirement watching television than before, for example, clocking nearly twenty-five hours per week (US News & World Report, June 25, 2010). A recent *Fortune* article described retirement this way: "It's extremely boring. We have built a fantasy in our minds that 20 years of free time is a dream come true. It's not."

Why am I telling you this? Because to live a fulfilling retirement, you need to be realistic and purposeful about what "down time" means to you—and what you want to do and accomplish. Having this vision and making it happen will contribute greatly to a rewarding retirement.

Prime Point 3: What is the right mix between planned and unstructured activities for me in retirement?

Throughout her career, Diane made sure she had interesting, challenging work assignments and she feels gratified by the work she does day to day as an executive of a nonprofit. However, recently she has found herself thinking more about retirement and looking forward to the opportunity to read, knit, play Scrabble, and spend time with her children and grandchildren. She had noticed that her priorities

Getting older can be a joy as we change from a frenetic work pace to a more leisurely lifestyle and our body acclimates to this new slower schedule.

have shifted and that pastimes she had regarded as a classic retirement cliché are sounding far better than they did two or three years ago. She is a little perplexed that she has evolved into this way of thinking. She finds herself wondering how—and when—did this happen. And she worries that she will "waste" her retirement.

Women need to give themselves a break. We have felt guilty for so long—kids, spouse, work, achieving perfection. As we reach our golden years, it is perfectly reasonable not only to start feeling liberated from past responsibilities, but to enjoy this new unstructured freedom.

In an effort to help you organize your retirement planning, we compiled a retirement decision inventory (RDI) for you to work through in order to gauge where you are in the process. The RDI is a great inventory of the decisions you need to make before and during retirement. Use it for planning what you need to do and also to revisit some of the decisions you may have made previously to see whether they are still in line with your retirement vision.

The RDI

Life/Work	
	How long will I stay at my current job?
	Do I want or need to work in retirement?
	If I work, do I work for myself or someone else?
	Should I volunteer? What makes me happy?
	Do I value and support something in my community that I want to give my time to?
	If I work, do I find a job related to my favorite hobby?
	What have I always dreamed of doing (work or play)?
	How much travelling do I want to do? And to where?
	How frequently should I visit my kids?
	How do I maintain my lifestyle in later retirement given I might have health constraints?
Health	
	Do I need to learn more about Medicare?
	How can I better manage my stress?
	Is my physical condition acceptable to me? (And if not, what do I need to do to be in shape?)

	Will my retirement income be enough to cover my health care and prescription costs?
	In what ways will I manage any chronic conditions I have or will develop (lifestyle changes, alternative medicine, regular checkups)?
	Do I need to (and how will I) change my eating habits?
	Am I financially prepared if my spouse or I will need nursing home care?
	Am I prepared if my spouse/partner dies?
	How do I want to die? Do I have an end-of-life plan written down?
Home	
	Can I pay off or pay down my mortgage now?
	Would I refinance my home to pay bills?
	Do I buy a more or less expensive home when I retire?
	Do I expand/make improvements to my current home that better fits my lifestyle?
	Can I afford a second home?
	Should I relocate to a more affordable city for retirees?
	Should I relocate to be closer to my family?
	Should I consider now whether I will need to move, live with my kids or in assisted living in late retirement?
	Who gets my home and possessions when I die?
	Do I have a will or living trust to seamlessly transfer home and property?
Family	
	Do my parents have enough saved for their health care?
	How can/should my parents pay for care—and what will be my role?
	What care choices should I recommend for my parents (assisted living, nursing home, in their home, my home)?
	What is my role in their end-of-life decisions?
	What are my views about end-of-life care?
	How much should I contribute to my children's or grandchildren's education? Should I help them pay off debt?
	How much of my time might go to care of a spouse or other family member?
	Should I volunteer to take care of my grandkids?
	What should I do to help my spouse live longer and be healthier?
	Is our living will or trust in place and up-to-date?
	Can I leave money to my kids/grandkids?

What did you learn? Did you find some areas which need more thought? Were you surprised at your answers to some of these questions?

Michelle and Andy met with their lawyer to update their wills, which included end-of-life decisions in the form of living wills and health care powers of attorney. Michelle was very clear that if she was ever in such a state that the doctors did not believe she would ever gain consciousness and function normally, she wanted her husband to "pull the plug" with no resuscitation. She was dumbstruck that Andy felt entirely different about his end-of-life plan. Andy did not want to die if even there was the most remote chance that he could recover. He wouldn't give consent to "pull the plug" under any circumstances. Knowing how strongly (and differently) her husband felt about the subject, Michelle decided to put her daughter in charge rather than her husband, should she be unable to communicate. Andy and Michelle learned a lot by talking about these difficult subjects and were able to come up with a plan that worked for both of them. This is not an easy conversation, but it is too important to leave to chance.

Women who are balancing work and family are constantly on a tight schedule, making sure their work deadlines are being met, households are running smoothly, and family members are taken care of. Most working women get used to this kind of schedule, so it can be quite a shock to find yourself in retirement with a great deal of free time on your hands. This can both be exhilarating and disturbing!

Once you've reflected on choices regarding some of your financial, family, and estate-planning issues, it's time to focus on how you will spend your retirement days. What type of retirement do you foresee? What kind of activities will keep you interested? What kind of involvement would you like to have with your former industry or profession, if any? Does a second career or part-time work intrigue you? What type of recreation do you enjoy? How does this all mesh with your partner or spouse's plans?

Another discussion that spouses might have is what to do if one becomes incapacitated (i.e., nursing home, home assistance, or something else). Most people who are above average income should put more of their assets into a trust so that the state can't go after them should a spouse have to be admitted into a nursing home.

Carolyn's dad always hated nursing homes and said so frequently. So when her mother had no recourse but to take him to a nursing facility once his Alzheimer's incapacitated him, she felt like she was betraying him. If they had discussed the subject and agreed on a resolution, it would have been a lot easier. Every (daily) visit reminds Carolyn's mother of her "betrayal." And she lives with guilt to this day.

In order to find happiness, it is important to match your skills and strengths to whatever you plan to spend your time doing. Next, we will look at what has given you the most fulfillment in your life and your work, and we'll analyze the skills you were using at the time. If, for instance, you really loved working with people and teams, you'll likely want to engage in activities or work with others during retirement. On the other hand, if you are most satisfied when you work on your own to accomplish something, you'll want to consider this as you plan your retirement activities. In the next chapter, we will turn our attention to crafting a retirement plan in a way that is invigorating, enjoyable, and suits your needs.

Let's get back to Maggie's story at the beginning of the chapter...

Maggie had established a successful brand and had a track record of effectiveness in her field, and although she had numerous employees who loved the company, none were viable candidates for buying it. Maggie decided there were various options in her exit planning. She elected to pursue individuals who had previously expressed interest in acquiring the company. Ideally, she'd like to find a like-minded but younger person to buy out or acquire the company through an acquisition. Maggie started the interview process and began meeting with individuals who fit her criteria. Because Maggie enjoyed working but was ready to spend more time with her family, she would work as long as the buyers needed it. She felt that by being available to the new buyers, she could support their initial needs in meeting clients and building relationships, all while lessening her responsibilities with the company and increasing her time spent with family away from the company. Maggie was confident that her exit plan would foster the kind of transition she envisioned, leading into her successful retirement.

Like success, change is many things to many people. With Positive Mental Attitude, change is a learning experience, a rung on the ladder, a plateau at which to get your thoughts in order and prepare to try again.
—W. Clement Stone

CHAPTER 2
Turning Change into Growth and Fulfillment

There is no doubt that retirement represents a significant life change, no matter what your plans are for the years ahead. You will likely be transitioning to a different level of activity, your daily routine will be new, you won't be seeing the same people you've worked with each day, your level of intellectual stimulation may decrease—and the list goes on. The stresses you experienced in your former job may be replaced with something different—anxiety about your transition from the traditional workforce to retirement. It is a big adjustment, even for those who have thought about the future and have put plans into place.

Many people have been locked in to their jobs and lifestyles for years, not necessarily enjoying them but reluctant to change and risk the unknown. Without realizing it, they may have gradually grown rigid and inflexible, which has impeded personal and professional growth.

The good news? Change can be positive, depending largely on whether we acknowledge it, accept it, and view it as a part of our growth. Within change, there is almost always opportunity: new friends, new insights, new work, and new experiences.

In addressing change constructively, we have to recognize a basic truth about human nature. All changes involve some uncertainty—and most people don't like uncertainty. This can create anxiety and stress even for the healthiest, best-adjusted people.

Julie has been completely engaged in her career for over thirty years and is, by every standard, a highly successful businesswoman. She has helped to grow and expand her company in a multitude of ways. When the subject of retirement comes up, she gets defensive and hurt, and you can see the stress spread across her face. She can't imagine life without the work she so deeply loves. So at age seventy, she is still actively working every day. However, after giving her future some hard thought and having a heart-to-heart with a close friend, she has begun to see that change is inevitable. She acknowledges that it will be to her benefit to make some decisions about whether and when she will retire and what she wants to be doing in the next few years. Although it will be tough, she knows that she needs to take control of her destiny and plan the next phase of her life.

How do you deal with change?

Many of us fall into one of the following categories when dealing with change. Which describes you best?

Resistance

A common reaction to change is to resist it. Do you get hostile and angry and direct a lot of negative energy toward thinking about events from the past? Or do you keep replaying things that happened, perhaps blaming yourself or someone else and taking your frustration out on family and friends? People often play the what-if game, asking themselves continually, "What if I had taken this direction, or this job, or relocated—or done something entirely different with my life?" These kinds of mind games ultimately sap the energy needed to move forward into a happy and successful retirement.

Advice: Acknowledge the past and move on! You have the future ahead of you.

Hopelessness

Are you one of the people who react to change passively? You may feel that you lost control of your career a long time ago, and so you've given up hope. If you wait for things to happen to you and expect less out of life, in the process, you often get less. Many women have not been as engaged in their careers as they could have been. They may have been promoted, assigned to new responsibilities, and moved around in their careers at the direction or suggestion of others. However well-intentioned these others have been, the result is that they gave up control.

Advice: It is important, at the preretirement planning stage of your life, to take back that sense of control. Resolve to put your future firmly in your hands. You are the steward of your career—no one else is.

Wheel Spinning

Does change cause you to launch into a flurry of activity—confusing motion with purpose—without taking time to plan or set priorities? If you engage in a retirement career search without being focused, you will feel like you are spinning your wheels—and you are! If you are unclear or unrealistic about what you want to do, others can't help you and you end up feeling frustrated. For example, if your goal is to join a board, consult or write a book, and you don't have the appropriate credentials or experience, you won't get anywhere.

Alyssa resigned from her company at age sixty-two to "write a book." She had always wanted to be an author and felt she had a lot to say. But as it turned out, it was a lot harder than she thought, and she had to rethink her plans.

Advice: Take a deep breath and think things out before you fly into motion. Put your plan on paper and see if it makes sense. Do a skills "gap" analysis on the skills you will need to achieve your ideal goal, and seek ways to fill those gaps with experiences now.

Procrastination

Does the idea of change immobilize you? Do you have ideas in your head but have difficulty putting them into action? Do you find yourself delaying your planning to do less important things? Enough excuses!

Advice: Get serious about the real work you have ahead of you. If you need help getting started, enlist a friend or a group of friends to spark you into action. Take little steps forward by setting deadlines and sticking to them in your planning, goal setting, networking.

To succeed in changing your life, it is vital that you know yourself, your likes and dislikes, your strengths and weaknesses, and the skills you possess. Most people have never taken the opportunity to slow down and evaluate their skill set, abilities, and personal strengths. Most of us are too busy during our career-building years to take a look back at what we've accomplished. We are so immersed in the daily fabric of our lives that we don't see the very patterns right in front of us. But this retrospective gives us important information in going forward. Information about your past helps you navigate the options for your future.

Now is the opportune time to step back and take a deeper look. And when you do—by working through this book and afterward—you will realize *you know more than you think.* Your apparent spur-of-the-moment past decisions actually drew upon consistent patterns of thinking, feeling, and acting. You were making choices over the years, both consciously and unconsciously, that both reflected and reinforced your likes and dislikes—in your relationships, in your way of thinking and making decisions, and even in the field or industry you chose.

In taking the time to recognize your personal patterns and preferences, you will see that they serve you well as useful and practical guides for asserting control over the future.

Jacey was unexpectedly fired after twenty-five years of a successful career in corporate communications with a large global advertising firm. After a year of dealing with her bitterness and fear, she started her own boutique communications and advertising company, and many of her old clients chose to work with her. Jacey realized after the first year of profitability that the termination from her previous firm was the best thing that ever happened to her!

For that reason, this book places high value on *knowing yourself* as an essential first step in planning your retirement and living in your prime. Once you have this focus, it will be easier to build a realistic structure for your retirement decisions. Then all you'll need is the energy to put it into action!

Facing Your Fears

How many people do you know who have retired? Take the time to try and recall their situations—how they made adjustments, issues they encountered, successes they achieved, rewards they experienced.

Cameron blithely moved into retirement without giving it much thought. After forty years of being a nurse in the oncology department in a major hospital, she assumed she would relish the free time to read books, organize her closets, and lunch with friends. Unfortunately, the initial glow of her newfound freedom soon wore off, and she was bored. She needed a plan B.

Perhaps look at your parents' retirement and those of their friends. Think about former bosses and colleagues who retired, or maybe even your neighbors or friends. What do you observe about their lives during retirement—do they seem content, are they engaged in activities, or do their lives seem isolated and lackluster?

Here are some specific questions to consider and an example for each.

- *Do you know someone who retired and took on a second career entirely different from his or her prior work life?*

<hr/>

<hr/>

Sadie, a clothing designer and entrepreneur, opened her first clothing store in suburban Philadelphia at the age of thirty. She quickly opened her second and third stores, building her business from the ground up and watching it flourish throughout her thirties and early forties. At fifty-two, she received an incredible offer to sell her business—and so she did. With her financial security taken care of by the sale of her company, she set about thinking about how she wanted to spend her time. She loved field hockey, which she played from an early age all the way through college. Having helped coach her own daughter's team, she always had the sport in her life and loved watching young girls develop their athletic skills. Sadie followed her heart and has reinvented herself as a field hockey coach at a private high school. She was also able to use her business acumen to start a series of summer camps for field hockey players of all ages. Her most notable achievement is a weekend camp in which the top field hockey players from all over the country came to be seen and recruited by some of the best college programs. Even though her "retirement" is incredibly different from her first career, she couldn't be happier!

- *Do you know people who dramatically changed their style of living— where they lived, their relationship with family and friends, their basic life priorities? How did it work out?*

<hr/>

<hr/>

Kay was an enthusiastic Francophile. She had always enjoyed French cooking and art, and she kept her language skills up-to-date as an adjunct French teacher at a local college during the summers. Upon retirement, she didn't hesitate for a moment about how or where she would spend her next years. She packed up and relocated to France in a small town about twenty minutes outside of Paris just three months after retiring. She quickly found a part-time job as a sous chef in a local three-star restaurant. She invites her friends and family to visit whenever they can since she has plenty of room in her two-bedroom flat not far from the many art galleries in Paris. She enjoys the French culture and the opportunity to connect with new and different people and feels truly rejuvenated by her new life.

- **Do you know of anyone who suffered health problems due to the stresses related to retirement? Do you know anyone whose health improved once they retired?**

_____

_____

Delores had been overweight for the better part of her adult life. Work and family habitually got in the way of her taking care of her own health. Every year, she made a New Year's resolution to start exercising and to eat more healthfully, but by February, she was back to her old habits. When she retired, she made it one of her top priorities to become healthy and fit. Her reasoning was that since she now had more time in her schedule, there was no more room for excuses. This was her new project! She started going to the gym with a neighbor three mornings a week and took walks with her husband after dinner. After talking with a nutritionist, she began visiting the local farmer's market once a week to buy fresh fruit and vegetables and began making some healthy new dishes. Not only has she lost over twenty-five pounds, but Delores—now age sixty-six—feels better than ever. In this case, retirement gave Delores the time and energy she needed to do something really important for herself—improving her own health.

- **Do you know of anyone whose marriage or family relationships improved after retirement?**

_____

_____

Tara is charismatic and genuine, and she enjoyed using her great people skills in her role as a regional director for a major bank. While she had always loved her job, it caused strains on her relationship with her children over the years because it seemed to take so much of her time and energy. She was constantly conflicted because although the work gave her a great deal of satisfaction, she wasn't able to spend the time she wanted with her kids. As she neared retirement, she became increasingly convinced that she wanted to resolve these tensions before it was too late. When the time came, Tara knew how she would spend her retirement—with her now-grown kids and their small children! So she is now happily engaged with her family, waiting at the bus stop each day at 3:00 p.m. and spending time with her grandkids until their parents return home from work. Her children are very grateful for her help and support, and everyone's quality of life has improved. Tara loves her new role and is relishing the deeper connections she is forging with her family. She feels it is never too late to make up for lost time!

- **What are some of the volunteer activities of the retired people you know?**

_____

_____

Mia, a retired history professor, volunteers three days a week to provide transportation for older people who need assistance because they are frail or disabled. She takes them to and from their doctor visits and other appointments, and it makes her feel incredibly good to help them. She enjoys talking with her "passengers" about the lives they've lived and experiences they've had and finds every day to be a new adventure as she soaks up a wealth of knowledge and insights into history. Mia's volunteer job is a great match with her background and interests.

What have you learned? Did you gain any insights by thinking about individuals you know who are retired? Hopefully, you are ready to answer the following questions.

- **Whose has been the most successful retirement you know of? What makes it successful in your eyes? Why?**

_____

_____

_____

- **Whose has been the least successful retirement? Why?**

_____

_____

_____

Unfortunately, we hear a lot of stories about individuals whose retirement has not turned out the way they envisioned it. We can learn much by thinking about the experiences of others and applying them to ourselves. By being thoughtful about the issues and, in essence, managing the process of your retirement, you greatly increase the opportunity to spend your retirement days in a very positive and satisfying place.

As this chapter ends, take a moment to reflect and jot down your thoughts so far based on what you have learned.

- **What will I *not* do based on what I have learned thus far?**

  Example: After talking with some friends who have regretted not having a retirement plan, I will not assume that relaxing and reading good books will satisfy me.

  _____

  _____

  _____

- **What are the top things I *need* to do based on what I've learned thus far?**

  Example: I need to interview colleagues and friends who have recently retired to find how they did it and how it's going.

  _____

  _____

  _____

Now that you've had an opportunity to look at various retirement outcomes and consider what you've learned along the way, we will work on assessing how your skills can be applied in retirement.

The person born with a talent they are meant to use will find their greatest happiness in using it.

—Johann Wolfgang von Goethe

CHAPTER 3
Discovering Your Skills and Talents

By understanding your greatest skills and abilities, you will have valuable information with which to plan your future. We'll help you identify the areas where you've been successful and have experienced satisfaction so that you can match them to your potential retirement activities. Though some of your skills and abilities are readily identifiable, others may be less obvious. The exercises on the next few pages will help.

Nancy, a regional bank vice president on the brink of retirement, wasn't sure where her next years would—or should—take her. She decided to review her history and do an analysis of her skills and strengths in order to gain clarity about what might be best for her. She soon realized she felt best about the middle part of her career, when she was a sales representative. She remembered her pleasure in connecting with others and building relationships with her customers. Her recent promotions had taken her away from all that. Though the skills she remembered enjoying the most were from earlier time, Nancy believed that a sales position might make sense for her future. She decided to explore the option of part-time sales, which she felt she might really enjoy.

When you connect your happiest career moments to the actual "things" you were doing at the time, you begin to realize what you enjoyed doing most at work.

The next few exercises will help you develop a heightened awareness of your personal and professional strengths and how they can help you reach your future goals. Putting your strengths and history on paper is also the first step to creating a "script" to use as you talk with friends and colleagues about your ideas for retirement.

Reviewing Your Career History

To get started, fill out the chart below by listing your professional career history, including the responsibilities for each position. This will help you think about some of the skills and abilities you have honed along the way.

Company	Position	Dates	Responsibilities

You should be very proud of what you've done in your career! Even though you may want to do something entirely different going forward, it is not only important to acknowledge the work you've done over the years but also to reflect upon your successes. Do you notice a theme in your progression of jobs? Because you were good in your work, did you receive regular promotions? And were you happy in your positions? If no, why? These are important questions to ask yourself as you reflect upon your career history.

Identifying Your Accomplishments

We all have experienced distinct moments of satisfaction after having accomplished something or after having a particularly rewarding experience. These may appear "ordinary" to others, but what matters is that *we* consider them important. Consider the definition of an accomplishment:

An accomplishment is something you enjoyed
doing, did well and found satisfying.

Spend a few minutes thinking about the top accomplishments in your personal and professional life. Think of five accomplishments. They may come from any time period, any facet, or any part of your life—personal or professional. Your accomplishments need not be related or interconnected in any way, but do try to be *as specific as possible in describing the accomplishment.* Here are some examples.

Too vague: Significantly increased company profits.

Specific: *Produced* record pretax profits in excess of $8.7 million, a 12 percent increase over the previous year, while positioning the company for expansion.

Too vague: Had two wonderful kids.

Specific: *Raised* two kids, who graduated from great colleges and have both launched their careers in their chosen field of study. We are close and still talk at least once a week.

Too vague: Went from supervisor to manager in two years.

Specific: *Was promoted* to manager after two years for my ability to lead a team through a difficult project and meet our financial targets at a difficult time.

Too vague: Entered into a transaction to provide for future growth for the company.

Specific: *Negotiated* a joint venture, which guided the company into a new $56 million market, enhancing the product line and ensuring continued growth with the addition of better technology.

Too vague: Finished a triathlon.

Specific: *Trained* for six months and *successfully completed* my first triathlon in the top 25 percent.

Don't be modest! This is not the time to be shy about what you have accomplished.

When Melissa reviewed her career history and her accomplishments, she remembered how happy she was early in her career when she interviewed prospective college students for a graduate program. She enjoyed listening to their stories and counseling them, and she felt she truly made a difference in their lives. As she thought about it, she realized she would like to be able to work with students during her retirement. She formed a small company to counsel college graduates who were just entering in their careers on how to identify work that will be satisfying and lead to success.

In the next section, list your top five career/personal accomplishments. Be specific and begin each accomplishment with an action verb. Give your age at the time of each accomplishment as well.

1. _____

_____

_____

_____

Age_____

2. _____

_____

_____

_____

Age_____

3. _____

_____

_____

_____

Age_____

4. _____

_____

_____

_____

Age_____

5. _____

_____

_____

_____

Age_____

How does that feel? Remember, these are the peak accomplishments in your life and career that you did well, enjoyed doing, and from which you gained satisfaction. You can assume you utilized strengths in achieving each of these accomplishments which uniquely define you and your capabilities. You will find that you use these same strengths again and again. It is these strengths that we need to identify and clarify.

Also ask yourself, were your top accomplishments spread throughout your career or bunched together? If they were all in one time period, this may indicate that the jobs before or after this time didn't draw upon your skills and strengths, a fact worth noting. When you truly reflect on your life thus far, it's pretty amazing to see all that you've achieved. Now is where we begin to interweave your past successes into a retirement plan that is equally as successful.

Assessing Your Skills

Based on your accomplishments, we are now going to make a list of the *abilities and skills* you used to achieve these. Specifically, we are going to evaluate the *motivated abilities* and *technical skills* you used to complete each accomplishment. First, let's review exactly what we mean.

A *motivated ability* is a nontechnical skill, ability, talent, or personal quality that comes from within you. Examples of these are planning, organizing, managing, problem solving, decision making, persuading, innovating, persevering, etc. You may have been born with this ability or developed it over the course of your career. *Motivated abilities* are usually present when you are doing your very best work and enjoying almost every minute.

A *technical skill* is a learned professional skill that you were either taught or which you learned on the job. Examples of these are data processing, financial analysis, marketing, banking, human resource management skills, etc. Sometimes, a technical skill is also a motivated ability like coaching, counseling, interviewing, organizing, etc. They are essential skills for your job but also innate to who you are as a person.

Using the next chart, list the abilities or skills you used to complete your accomplishments in the left-hand column. The list on the left can be as long as necessary. Start with accomplishment 1 and think of all the skills and abilities you used. For example, if in your accomplishment you used *creative thinking* skills and you used *problem solving* skills, you would write each of these skills in a box on the left-hand side and put an *x* under accomplishment 1 for each. See the example. Continue with accomplishment 1, listing all the skills and strengths you applied when performing this accomplishment.

Example

Abilities and Skills	Accomplishments					Total Score
	1	2	3	4	5	
Creative Thinking	x		x			2
Problem Solving	x	x		x		3
Collaborating	x	x	x	x	x	5

Need help thinking of your motivated and technical skills? Try some of these:

Skills

Administering	Collaborating	Directing
Advising	Communicating	Documenting
Alleviating	Computing	Editing
Allocating	Conceptualizing	Educating
Analyzing	Conducting	Engineering
Appraising	Consulting	Establishing
Arbitrating	Controlling	Evaluating
Arranging	Convincing	Executing
Assessing	Coordinating	Experimenting
Auditing	Counseling	Facilitating
Bargaining	Creating	Forecasting
Budgeting	Delegating	Fund-raising
Building	Demonstrating	Guiding
Calculating	Designing	Helping
Caring	Developing	Hiring
Coaching	Diagnosing	Identifying

Implementing	Modifying	Resolving
Improving	Motivating	Revising
Improvising	Negotiating	Scheduling
Influencing	Organizing	Searching
Informing	Persuading	Selecting
Initiating	Planning	Selling
Innovating	Presenting	Setting goals
Inspiring	Presiding	Solving
Instructing	Producing	Speaking
Interviewing	Programming	Supervising
Inventing	Publicizing	Systemizing
Investigating	Reading	Teaching
Leading	Reconciling	Testing
Making	Recruiting	Theorizing
Managing	Refining	Training
Marketing	Reorganizing	Troubleshooting
Mediating	Representing	Understanding
Merchandising	Researching	Writing

After you have listed all the skills and abilities for accomplishment 1, check the respective box for each and move on to accomplishment 2. First, determine whether you used any of the skills from accomplishment 1 in accomplishment 2. If so, put an *x* next to each skill under accomplishment 2. Then add the additional skills that were unique to accomplishment 2 and check those boxes. For example:

- Did you use "planning" in multiple accomplishments? Put an *x* under each accomplishment in which you used "planning."
- Did you use your "persuasion" abilities in different capacities? Put an *x* under each accomplishment in which your "persuasion" ability allowed you to succeed.

After you have thoughtfully considered the skills and abilities that have contributed to your various accomplishments, tally up how many times you utilized each specific skill and ability in the right-hand column.

Abilities and Skills	Accomplishments					Total Score
	1	2	3	4	5	

Which skills or abilities have the highest number in the right-hand column? What has this exercise revealed about how you have achieved your most important or memorable accomplishments? Do the skills and abilities you've used the most surprise you—or are they what you knew all along? How have they contributed to your development and expertise? If you find that you consistently used several skills and/or abilities, they are likely to be the ones you'll want to emphasize in your retirement since you have been most successful—and happiest—when you have used them in achieving your most satisfying and enjoyable accomplishments.

When Lindsay was asked in a graduate class to describe her greatest strengths, she was dumbstruck. As she began to rack her brain for the answers, she realized she could easily describe the strengths of her friends and colleagues but was uncomfortable talking about her own. In that moment, she understood that she needed to set aside some time to think through her successes and the strengths she used to accomplish them so she could easily bring these strengths to mind and share them with others.

Summarizing Your Strengths

Let's summarize your results from the previous exercise. In the space below, rank your *motivated abilities* in the order of most frequent occurrence.

Begin with the motivated ability that received the highest number in the right-hand column.

1. _____

2. _____

3. _____

4. _____

5. _____

Now, in these spaces below, rank your *technical skills*—those skills that you have learned and perfected on the job.

1. _____

2. _____

3. _____

4. _____

5. _____

Now, select your six greatest strengths from these two lists. Consider the satisfaction you get from using these strengths, your level of experience and expertise, and their marketability in making your final selection.

1. _____ 2. _____

3. _____ 4. _____

5. _____ 6. _____

Remember, when you were most satisfied and happy with your work, you were using these top six skills! Appreciating this fact alone is one of the remarkable findings in the above exercise. More importantly, if you continue to use these skills and abilities in your retirement, you *will* be successful! And happy! If alternatively, you find work that taps into your weakness, you will likely be unhappy and unsuccessful. (If you choose to do so, you can use this same exercise to analyze your failures and identify your weaknesses.)

Now we can begin to organize your greatest strengths in sentence form by writing a profile describing you and your greatest strengths. For example: *I am a creative, highly organized, marketing expert with over fifteen years in designing and implementing marketing plans for a financial services company. I am a team player, an excellent problem solver, and have strong financial expertise. I always meet my targets and timetables.*

My Summary Profile

_____

_____

_____

_____

_____

Though it may sound simple, this is not an easy description to write. You may not be used to talking about your strengths. However, being specific about who you are and what you do well is essential to prepare for the conversations you will have as you uncover future opportunities. The friends and professional contacts you talk with are going to need to hear an accurate and positive summary from you about your experiences, strengths, and skills in order to help you further your goals.

Now, let's expand your thinking and create a summary paragraph covering your career history in a few concise sentences.

I have over thirty years of talent management, recruiting, and compensation and benefits experience. In 2005, I was recruited by World Plus Company to manage the human resources function to include talent management, recruiting, and the HRIS system. I brought ten years of experience in consulting prior to that. I began my career as a recruiter with Herald Consulting.

My Career History

_____

_____

_____

_____

_____

Let's go back to your accomplishments. Be crisp and begin each with an active verb.

My greatest accomplishments were developing a total compensation strategy, reinforcing pay for performance and strategic goals, designing a performance management process linking individual goals with strategic and operating goals, and executing an incentive compensation plan to attract talent and drive profitable revenue growth.

Some of My Greatest Accomplishments

_____

_____

_____

_____

_____

_____

Finally, what are you looking for? Though you may not know precisely, others can help steer you by providing direction and advice. You might say, for example . . .

I am beginning to look ahead at my own personal retirement and would like to move into part-time work in the next few years. I am meeting with friends and colleagues in my network to get some new ideas as to how I might put my experience and strengths to work.
or
I have the opportunity to retire in two years but have decided that I would like to continue working, but doing something slightly different.
or
I would like to do voluntary work in the health-care industry upon my retirement such as . . . What do you think?
or

I don't know what I am looking for, but I would like to use the strengths that have made me successful so far. Do you have any ideas?

This is a pivotal stage in moving forward, so think about the general area you are interested in and frame the next question.

What Are You Looking For?

_____

_____

_____

_____

Now, put it all together.

My Summary Profile

_____

_____

_____

_____

_____

My Career History

_____

_____

_____

_____

_____

My Greatest Accomplishments

_____

_____

_____

_____

_____

What I Am Looking For

_____

_____

_____

_____

You may be surprised to uncover the many—sometimes forgotten—skills you developed over the course of your career. After working through your strengths and developing this script, you are ready to start talking to friends and colleagues about retirement.

Begin practicing this script and get it to a point where it's comfortable and easy to talk about. Remember, you are *collecting* information not making a decision. In addition, listening and being open to suggestions are key components to a successful conversation with someone who is trying to help.

You have done an important analysis of your professional career, and hopefully uncovered the things that you can do well and that give you enjoyment and satisfaction. These are the skills you want to carry into your future retirement role. The next chapter will discuss how to identify your contacts and approach them with your networking script.

It's all about people. It's about networking and being nice to people and not burning any bridges.

—M. Davidson

CHAPTER 4
Building Relationships

Now that you've had a chance to develop and refine your networking script, and perhaps practice with a few trusted friends, it is time to start thinking about how to approach others who may be able to help you.

First, let's take a look at how you feel about networking and where you stand on the subject. Do you enjoy networking? How do your relationship-building skills rate? Take the following quiz and see.

		Yes	No
1.	Do you have a positive attitude about networking?		
2.	Do you believe networking has value for you in reaching your retirement goals?		
3.	Are you open to networking opportunities?		
4.	Have you considered what your goals might be for networking?		
5.	Do you make an effort to have at least one networking meeting a week?		
6.	Do you build relationships with a variety of people?		
7.	Do you network with thought leaders, experts, and business competitors?		
8.	Do you network with people who are not close friends or coworkers?		

9. Do you give as much information and assistance in your networking as you take?		
10. Are you willing to make the time necessary to build relationships?		

If you answered yes to five or more questions, it sounds like you are on the right track. If you answered yes to fewer than that, you may need to reassess your strategy.

You might find that gearing up for the networking part of your retirement career search is the most difficult part for you. If you aren't a natural networker, you may need to be persuaded as to its benefits and learn some techniques on how to do it successfully.

The Power of Strategic Networking

While strategic networking and relationship building require time and effort, there are many rewards. As you consider your networking strategy, you'll want to think about three important groups who are vital to your future. The first group is your *key inner network*—people you know well and feel comfortable with. This group includes close friends and work colleagues. They may also be people you are friendly with through local associations, your neighborhood, church or synagogue, or perhaps through recreational activities.

The second "connection" category is your *key professional contacts*. This group includes your supervisors, peers, direct reports, and vendors or clients with whom you do business. Professional contacts are people both inside and outside your own organization.

The third "connection" category is your *broad network*—people who are two or three degrees away from you. Interestingly, these are sometimes the individuals who are able to give you the most insight because they can be more objective.

Dana was looking for a part-time fund-raising opportunity at a nonprofit organization when she found out that her neighbor, Jane, volunteers at the local library. She made a point of talking with Jane and found out about a new initiative in the works—a fund-raising campaign that was being launched to build a new

46

wing for the library. Dana was interested in learning more, and Jane referred her to the library's director of development. When Dana met with the director, she found that there was a temporary fund-raising position available—and the wheels were set in motion for getting Dana an interview.

In this example, it took a two-step process to get to the opportunity Dana was interested in. First, going to her neighbor, and then obtaining the referral to someone else in her broader circle—the library director.

"By the time I networked with twenty people in my broad circle of contacts, I captured three times that number of referrals. My network has really grown!"

Many people think that networking is synonymous with looking for a job, and since 80 percent of positions are uncovered through networking, clearly there is truth in this. In fact, it is very possible that your contacts will lead you to a job opportunity now or in the future. However, there are many other possible benefits in making contacts, including the following:

- Gaining valuable information and ideas
- Becoming better known
- Learning interpersonal and leadership skills
- Building allies and developing reciprocal relationships
- Brainstorming ideas/solving problems
- Acquiring new opportunities and leads
- Understanding various organizations
- Assessing your worth on the job market
- Discovering a community or professional group of interest
- Being asked to join a board or committee

Did you ever think networking could benefit you in so many ways?

Identify Your Key Inner Network

In the following exercise, you will list the people within your key inner network who are important to you and the relationship you have with them. These are your personal contacts—people who know you well and are genuinely interested in your success. This list includes your closest confidants, your relatives, friends, and other people who offer insight about your retirement goals.

In the chart below, list your contacts within the appropriate categories, along with information about each person and your relationship with them, how often you see each other, and any special information you might have. We've given you a sample chart with some ideas.

My Key Inner Network (example)

Category	Name	Position	Current Relationship	Frequency of Contact	Special Interests	Next Steps
Friends	Chelsea Martin	Consulting firm partner	Members of the same book club	About 9x a year	She likes to read nonfiction.	Ask her to lunch.
Relatives	Shane Smith	CIO of manufacturing business	Brother-in-law	Twice a month	My nephew—his son!	Arrange time to talk.
Neighbors	Chris James	Sales manager for a competitor	Lives two doors down from me	Every week or so	Has a dog same breed as mine	Walk dogs together.
Former Work Colleagues	Lucy Mifflin	Sales	Members of the same women's organization	Every month	She's a workaholic and could use a break.	Ask to have coffee.
School Buddies	Erin Meredith	Professor	See every summer	Several times a year	Alumni club officer for my college	Set aside one-on-one time.
Acquaintance— Religious Affiliation/ Sports Club/ Mom Group	Whitney Beach	Financial advisor	Know through church	See about twice a month	She has two little girls whom she adores.	Invite her over.

Now, fill out the second chart with your key inner network contacts to see who you should be connecting with to help you navigate your retirement plan.

My Key Inner Network						
Category	Name	Position	Current Relationship	Frequency of Contact	Special Interests	Next Steps
Friends						
Relatives						
Neighbors						
Former Work Colleagues						
School Buddies						
Acquaintance through Religious Affiliation/ Sports Club/ Mom Group						
Others?						

Identify Your Key Professional Network

Trish and her boss Ken had worked together for over ten years, and Trish had shared with him some of her retirement plans and goals. She had spent a great deal of time assessing her skills and interests. She knew that ideally she wanted to stay in her field, though in a different capacity and with fewer hours. As her retirement date approached, Ken suggested it might be beneficial for Trish to schedule a meeting with his boss, the division head, to discuss the situation and get some candid feedback. The division head was so impressed with Trish's analysis and focus that she told Trish she would like her to stay with the company in a part-time role. Trish was thrilled that she could achieve her retirement dream by changing roles in her present company.

The people you work with every day know you well and are often a great source for leads and advice. Whether you plan to retire in the near term or in a few more years, it serves you well to enhance your relationships with key work colleagues.

In the following exercise, you will list the people within your key professional network who are important to you and the relationship you currently have with them. Your key professional circle includes contacts who have a stake or interest, personally or professionally, in the success or failure of your plans and goals for retirement.

Once you develop your list, you will have a better idea of steps needed to expand and maintain your relationships. Be creative in thinking about your key professional contacts. Ask yourself—who inside or outside of my company do I need to know? Who needs to be aware of my experience, skills, and abilities? What relationship would I like to have with the people listed, and what should I do to make it happen? This first chart has some examples.

My Key Professional Network (example)					
Category	**Name**	**Current Relationship/ Status**	**Why Network?**	**Relationship Desired**	**Next Steps**
Superior (s)	Henry Jones	Boss's boss. No informal contact, only see at biweekly meetings	Very influential	More comfortable level of interaction, more casual and regular	Stop in office once a month to update him, send e-mails or articles on pertinent topics

Peer (s)	Kate Reilly	Runs community investment department at my company	Highly regarded, her opinion of me is important.	More regular contact and exchange of ideas/info	Call to ask her to lunch; share my goals with her.
Client (s)	Clara Monroe	I participate in client meetings with her. Know her formally.	She is an important client and very vocal, so her opinion counts.	Warmer, more casual interaction	Get to client meetings earlier to have informal conversations with her. (I would love to work for her in retirement!)
Professional Advisors (CPAs, MDs, lawyers)	Candy Matlok	Prominent surgeon at major hospital	Is a lifelong member of our community and has lots of knowledge on nonprofits	Establish a friendship; find a community project that we can both get involved in.	Ask her to have coffee next week.
Direct Reports	Elena Griffin	Reports to me	Young, provides insight into the younger scene	Maintain our good relationship	Take her to lunch once a month.
Vendor(s)	Krista Winter	Sold us our payroll system. See quarterly.	Seems fun, and knows a lot about the community and kids' organizations	More casual and frequent interaction	See if we can set up a playdate for our grandchildren
Consultant (s)	Lora Kim	Works with human resources	She has an excellent pulse on the corporate field.	Maintain our good relationship	Ask her to coffee next month.

| Competitors | Kim Zwick | Head of sales | We know of one another. | One to two times a year at conferences | Need to research |
| Gurus/ Thought Leaders | Alex Berns | Sales trainer and book author | She knows most of the top sales-people in the country. | One good networking meeting | Arrange for an introduction by my CEO. |

This second chart is for you to complete. Think strategically about who can help you reach your retirement goals, and plan to make the meetings happen!

My Key Professional Contacts					
Category	Name	Current Relationship/Status	Why Network?	Relationship Desired	Next Steps
Superior (s)					
Peer (s)					
Client (s)					
Professional Advisors (CPAs, MDs, lawyers)					
Direct Report(s)					
Vendor(s)					
Consultant(s)					
Competitor(s)					
Gurus/Thought Leaders					

Broadening Your Network

Now that you have your key professional contacts, let's add to the list the third category—your broad network. This will help you begin to understand where your greatest networking potential lies, and its importance cannot be underestimated. Throughout the years, I have seen many examples of people who, while they are very successful in their careers, have spent virtually no time meeting people and participating in activities outside of work. When the time came that they needed contacts and visibility, they found themselves at square one. Most of these individuals regretted their situations and were determined not to let this happen again.

Remember, everyone is a potential contact in the context of broad networking—friends of friends, neighbors, professional acquaintances, former colleagues, and/or acquaintances from religious affiliations or sports clubs, anyone!

List people you'd like to add to your broad network and the steps you will take to further those relationships. Think of people one to two degrees away from you who might be useful in reaching your own specific retirement goal. The first chart below gives you some examples. Use the second chart to list the people you should get to know better.

My Broad Network (example)			
Category	**Name/Current Relationship**	**Value of Expanded Relationship**	**Next Steps**
Work Colleagues	Charlotte Kelly in accounting; don't know her	She's active in community organizations and can help me connect.	Call her to set up an introductory meeting.
Community Leaders	Sandy Smith, head of Pets for Life	She knows almost everyone! And I am interested in working with animals.	Go to her next fund-raiser and introduce myself.
Political Leaders	Melissa Caro, my state representative	She's well connected. May be able to give me contacts with local and state representatives who support animal rights	Write to her to introduce myself and my organization.

Conference Attendees	Megan Williams and Sarah Boyer, two women I met at last year's annual marketing conference	Both women were well connected in the marketing world and had superior reputations. Could be insightful about how to start my own business or freelance at a small firm	E-mail them and set up a date to grab a drink and talk business.
Others I would like to know?			

Think hard as you develop your own list. You might be surprised at the number of contacts you already have.

My Broad Network			
Category	Name/Current Relationship	Value of Expanded Relationship	Next Steps
Work Colleagues			
Community Leaders			
Political Leaders			
Conference Attendees			
Others I would like to know?			

Now that you've made your list and divided it into categories, ask yourself the following questions:

- Do I have a variety of contacts, or does most of my network fall within one or two categories?
- Do I have gaps that I need to fill?
- How often am I staying in touch with people I've listed?
- How open and diverse is my network?

Ideally, strategic networks are "open," meaning you have many contacts outside your functional area and/or company and "diverse," putting you in contact with people who are different from you professionally, ethnically, and gender-wise. Open and diverse networks usually result in more opportunities than those that are more one-dimensional. Even though expanding your reach beyond the "usual suspects" may feel like a bit of a stretch, it is worth doing—you'll soon find yourself getting new information and fresh ideas. If you only surround yourself with people who work where you do, live where you live, and think like you, you will limit yourself. The more diverse your network, the more opportunities are created.

"When I analyzed my network, I was surprised—and a little taken aback—to see that everyone listed had a similar background to mine. I thought I was much more connected to a larger and more diverse community. "

Do a Diversity Check!

Take a look at your inner network, your professional network, and your broad network. For every person listed, put a dot in one of the categories on the pie chart. You may end up having two dots for one person. See how open and diverse your network really is—and consider introducing yourself to people who are different from you. You will be amazed at how rich and helpful those conversations can be.

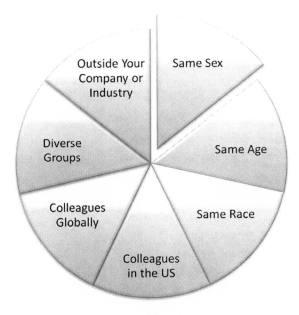

If you have found that your network is not as open and diverse as you'd like, get to work on building new relationships with people who are different from you and have had different experiences, and plan to monitor progress in six months. Think about people you haven't considered before and reassess the possible value of including them in your circle.

Tips for Networking Meetings

As you begin to embark on your networking meetings, here are some tips to help them go smoothly.

- Before your meeting, do some background investigative work on the person you are meeting with to find mutual connections and interests. LinkedIn.com is a good place to start. Also, see if you can find out a little about the individual's personality from someone who knows him or her in order to understand what to expect.
- Think about what you'd like to gain from the meeting, how to begin, and where the conversation might go. Your personality type will have an impact on style and delivery. If you are more on the introverted side, give special attention to rehearsing introductions and preparing questions in advance. If you are an extrovert, it is especially important to focus and be strategic so you don't dominate the conversation and do listen to what is being said.
- Use the first few minutes of the meeting to take any pressure off your contact and put him or her in a comfort zone. Give a brief summary of your background and the reason for the meeting. It is always best to write down what you plan to say and rehearse it. Remember to emphasize that you are looking for information and advice, not a job.
- Be aware of the clock! Establish up front how much time you have, and move on to the purpose of the meeting in a timely manner after the opening pleasantries.
- After your meeting, try to reconnect every four to six weeks by e-mail, phone, or letter, and let your contact know that you're working on

When Abbey did one of her six-week "loopback" calls, her contact mentioned he had heard that very day about an interesting opportunity. Abbey knew she wouldn't have been top of mind if she hadn't touched base! Good thing she had!

whatever the two of you talked about. For example, if you were given a referral, let him or her know that you have actually gotten in touch with the person. People will remember you for about four to six weeks—after that, you fall off their radar screen. Keep their psychological investment in you going!

Eight Ways to Keep Your Network Vibrant

1. Stay in regular communication with contacts.
2. Think about ways to refine your approach to networking.
3. Be receptive to introductions and requests for meetings.
4. Look for new avenues for networking.
5. Host networking events and meetings.
6. Be a "connector" who brings people together.
7. Find opportunities to be helpful to your contacts.
8. Stay in touch with contacts through all available communication tools (meetings, e-mails, voicemails, texts, etc.).

These principles will ensure your relationships stay vibrant and useful as you continue building your network.

When setting up a meeting, use the name of the person who referred you, and state the reason for the meeting. Better yet, have your mutual acquaintance e-mail or call ahead. If no one has referred you, it's more difficult to get a meeting with an important person—but not impossible. When you reach out to him or her, identify who you are by saying, "I'd like a few minutes of your time to discuss . . ." or "I'm interested in XYZ Organization, and since you're on the board, I'd like to get your perspective . . ." or "I heard you speak at a recent meeting and would like your advice on . . ." Be creative!

Getting Involved in Organizations and Activities

There are many reasons why women, especially those who are within several years of retirement, should consider getting more involved in a community organization or extracurricular activity. It is important to be an advocate, help others, make your voice heard, and contribute. Volunteering expands your network and influence and is a wonderful source of contacts with whom to explore retirement options. It is also a great way to contribute to a cause that you feel strongly about.

Let's review all the ways you can contribute to a community organization as well as learn from the experience.

What You Can Offer a Community Organization
- Advice and input for events, fund-raising
- Financial savvy and guidance
- Technical help in how to manage database client and donor information
- Contacts for resources and donations
- Leadership experience and enthusiasm for driving initiatives

What You Can Gain by Becoming Involved
- Exposure and visibility
- Team-building skills through leading projects and initiatives
- Networking skills honed by making introductions for the organization
- Personal satisfaction through helping a worthwhile cause
- Connections to people with whom you share common interests

As Kaley approached sixty-five and retirement, she called together a small group of friends who worked and were about her age. She asked them if they would find it beneficial to create a "support group" to help one another transition into retirement. There was a resounding "yes!" to her question and they planned their strategy. Each woman assessed her strengths, interests and possible options before the next meeting, and shared them with the group for feedback and advice. They met every other week and all of the participants received encouragement as they articulated - and then began to pursue their dreams. One year later, the group is still engaged. They have taken in some new members and are enjoying the satisfaction of helping one another reach their goals.

When you serve on a committee or board of an organization, you become a representative for the group. At an organization event or activity, consider yourself one of the hosts and make yourself accessible. Introduce yourself to those you don't know, be prepared to answer questions about the organization, and be enthusiastic about the cause. Stimulating interest in your organization is an important part of being involved and a great way to meet new people.

Are you involved enough in outside activities?

In order to gauge your current level of activities, take the following quiz.

	Yes	No
1. Do you use your skills and experience to help community and civic organizations?		
2. Do you sit on any boards of outside organizations?		
3. Have you carved out time outside of work to volunteer?		
4. Are you a working member of a professional, civic, or charitable organization?		
5. Do you consider volunteer work to be a part of your retirement plan?		
6. Do you have an active network of contacts outside of your business and personal friends?		
7. Do you engage in extracurricular activities that build contacts?		
8. Are you receptive when asked to participate in outside civic and community activities?		
9. Do you make it known that you are available to participate in outside activities or join boards?		

If you've answered yes to more than five of the above questions, you're doing some good work to raise your community profile. Four yeses? Though you have some things going, you may want to step up your activities. Less than four? You are probably not taking advantage of opportunities that will help you down the road.

Staying Organized

Once you've accumulated contacts from a broad range of meetings and activities and listed and categorized each individual, you need a solid system to keep you up-to-date with your follow-ups. This can be achieved by creating a database that tracks meeting dates, has room for notes and information, and jogs your memory on follow-ups. You can set this up on your computer using Excel or a similar spreadsheet.

Stay organized by updating it regularly!

My Contact Notes (example)

Name	Title	Date of Contact	Referral Source	Contact Summary	Future Strategy	Referred To
Grace Stanton	Starlight Bank, One Liberty Sq., Baltimore, MD Phone: 302-233-3300 E-mail: Stanton@ Starlight. com	3/9/12	Jack Bauer, EVP	Good meeting at her office about possible speaking opps, is pres. of Bankers Assoc. (Same birthday as mine!)	Call in May to discuss program for future meeting	Matt Daimler, another possible speaker
Matt Daimler	Lorien Company, 4400 West Blvd., Towson, MD Phone: 302-876-5000 E-mail: MLD@ LoComp. com	3/30/12	Grace Stanton	Phone call, left message	Try again in three days	

Fill out *your* contacts on this second form which you can also create on your computer.

My Contact Notes						
Name	Title	Date of Contact	Referral Source	Contact Summary	Future Strategy	Referred To

As you set up your own networking system, you may want to grade your contacts as As, Bs, or Cs, with A being the most influential people and C the least influential or your closest friends. To get started, try your networking skills on your C list folks—you may be pleasantly surprised by their insights and advice, and you have less to lose if the meeting doesn't go well. Get comfortable with your introduction and description of your skills and accomplishments—and then move higher up on your list to the Bs and As.

Connecting with Contacts

Developing a strategy for connecting with each contact will help you use your time effectively and maximize your interactions. Here are some ideas for making these connections.

- Set up a breakfast or lunch to discuss a topic of mutual interest.
- Invite a contact to attend an event at which you are a speaker, panelist, or guest.
- Send an article, book suggestion, or other piece of news your contact may find of value.
- Use LinkedIn as a resource to share information, introduce colleagues, and connect through groups of interest.
- Attend a meeting or event if someone you want to meet will be present. If necessary, use one of your contacts to get invited.
- Use Facebook to share articles or videos you come across or tips you know your network would appreciate.
- Join a professional women's group—some groups require that you have a job, so in retirement it may be more difficult to join. Join now!

Once you understand more about the individual you're meeting with, you'll be able to find ways to build your relationship. So when you're talking with someone, listen carefully and try to uncover useful information that will enable you to follow up.

Using LinkedIn as a Networking Tool

LinkedIn is a social media platform designed specifically for professional adults to seek advice, discuss current topics and events, pursue job or partnership opportunities, learn about other business practices, and so much more. Like Facebook, LinkedIn allows you to connect with those in your network, post articles, "like" comments or discussions; but unique to LinkedIn is that you can only connect with people you actually know or have a real connection with—whether that is a work connection, alumni connection, mutual connection with a colleague, or a friend you have met along the way.

LinkedIn strengthens and extends your existing network of trusted colleagues and was designed with business professionals in mind. With the ability to create a professional profile with your career history, degrees, areas of expertise, and personal summary, once you become a member, the social media site can be a wealth of information and potential networking opportunities. We suggest that you keep your profile up-to-date so that interested parties can check you out and join groups that interest you—share your knowledge and ask questions. Be an active member!

Women and Networking

Maintaining, growing, and nurturing your network takes time—something that most of us find in short supply. Even with the best of intentions, you can find yourself passing up solid networking opportunities because of other priorities. However, it is important to rethink this. Go out to lunch! Join that committee! Get out of your office!

In order to give yourself the best chance for success in retirement, networking now has to remain a top priority. Accept it as an integral and important part of your life. As you begin to see the rewards that networking brings, you will want to invest time in it whenever you can. Try to have at least two networking meetings a week, ideally face-to-face.

The unique communication style of women can be a strong asset in networking. Women are known to be empathetic and good listeners, traits which enable us to forge strong bonds.

One rainy Saturday, two mothers—Jessica and Heather—sat watching their sons play lacrosse and started talking. It happened that Jessica was one of the top women at a large international company. As their conversation continued, Heather sensed Jessica's unease as she talked about her job. Heather took the opportunity to tell Jessica she was a career counselor and offered her services if she was ever in need. Turns out, she was. Soon after they met, Jessica called Heather in the middle of a career crisis, which Heather guided her through. A couple of years later, Jessica was able to return the favor by recommending Jessica for an important project in her company.

Yet while you may possess these strengths, many women have challenges in other areas, such as assertiveness, self-promotion, or focused communication. Here are several things to keep in mind:

- Present yourself professionally: a polished appearance will help you feel confident and self-assured.
- Use powerful, effective language: a crisp delivery will boost your poise and authority.
- Be knowledgeable about what is going on in your community, industry, or area of expertise.
- Keep your eye on the goal: always focus on who you're talking with, how they can help you, and vice versa.

Don't underestimate the value of networking now and in the future. You never know who might be a future client or friend, a person with great ideas, or a connector to someone you want to meet. The more you build relationships with people, the more opportunity you will have to realize your retirement dreams. Use every opportunity offered you—on the playing field of your grandchild, in line at your local Starbucks, at a party, or during a break at a meeting. Don't forget the power of reciprocity, and always ask what you can do for those you network with. In the next chapter, we will look at how to dream, plan for, and cultivate a retirement that fulfills your desires and goals.

Every retiree in America will enjoy
on average over 6,000 sunrises.

CHAPTER 5

Considering Your Retirement Options—
The Sky's The Limit!

With people living longer and healthier lives, there are more options for retirement than ever before. This is both good news and bad because though in many ways "the sky's the limit," deciding on what you'd like to do can become challenging with so many possibilities to consider. Now that you've assessed what you're good at, the things that make you happy, and how to utilize your network, it's time to consider your retirement options.

"My work in public relations and marketing immediately led me to a consulting opportunity when I left full-time work. My experience, contacts in the industry, and solid reputation all worked to help me make this transition."

The Over-Fifty Workforce

In 1996, the percentage of workers in the United States age 50 and over was 20 percent, but that number is rising and, according to AARP, is now about 31 percent. Many businesses are recognizing the benefits of people who are more mature and stable. For years, job seekers were doing anything to look younger, but one recruiter we spoke to said he often looked for "gray hair" in job candidates. Though the media appears to be obsessed with youth, we second Betty Friedan's comment, "Aging is not 'lost youth' but a new stage of opportunity and strength." Let's look at some of the advantages older workers bring to the table. These are some assets that you can stress in your meetings with contacts or in future interviews:

- Experience
- Stability and maturity
- Lower cost on pension
- Lower cost on medical
- Wisdom from experience
- Appreciative attitude
- Strong work ethic
- Flexibility on schedule and pay

According to a recent AARP article, some of the top industries seeking older workers include advocacy, working with children, conservation, teaching, community safety, and local or global poverty alleviation. In addition, according to the CIA World Factbook, the average life expectancy for American women was 80.8 years in 2010, meaning soon-to-be retirees could spend 20+ years in retirement. Twenty years is a long time, and we believe you could have a lot more fun if you spend those years doing something you enjoy and find satisfying. If you need to supplement your income with either part-time or full-time work, combining work with pleasure *and* pay should be the goal.

"I was surprised to find that when I interviewed for certain positions, they were actually looking for someone my age. Of course, many jobs are clearly geared toward younger people, and I will cross those off my list so I don't get discouraged."

As you go through this chapter and contemplate the various options available, be sure you are taking into consideration the information you've gathered so far. Let's review where we are.

- What are your top three retirement options?

1. _____

2. _____

3. _____

- What were the skills and strengths you used when you were the happiest in your career?

_____

_____

_____

- How do they match the options most appealing to you?

_____

_____

_____

- What decisions have you and your spouse made about where to live and how?

_____

_____

_____

- Have you analyzed your network? Can it support one of your preferred options and how?

_____

_____

_____

- Which option will provide the kind of growth and fulfillment you seek and why?

_____

_____

_____

Let's review the following six categories of post-career employment:
- Self-Employed/Entrepreneurial
- Second/Retirement Career
- Part-Time/Full-Time Consulting Work
- Volunteering/Service Activities
- Board Participation (Paid and Nonpaid)
- Social/Leisure/Family Activities
- Teaching/Coaching

Self-Employed/Entrepreneurial

Research indicates that 30 percent of people in career transition will exercise the option of self-employment. And while the freedom of being your own boss can be exhilarating, a staggering 50 percent of all new businesses fail within the first year (US Small Business Administration), so it is extremely important to gauge whether you have the right "stuff" to go out on your own—or whether it's the right decision for your circumstances.

As Elizabeth began networking in the search for meaningful retirement work, she noticed that the first reaction of a number of people she spoke with was to tell her to start her own business. Although she agreed that her skills and experience for health-care consulting could be a great fit, she knew she needed and wanted full-time work and the security of a regular paycheck. She determined that she needed to communicate better in her meetings to make sure her colleagues and friends understood her goals. That way, she reasoned, they could open their minds to additional possibilities for her. Elizabeth stayed on course after making a conscious effort to communicate her goals better and found her meetings much more helpful.

There are a number of business possibilities to explore if you are interested in being an entrepreneur:
- Consulting
- Buying or buying into an existing business
- Buying a franchise
- Starting a new franchise/business
- Getting involved in a "start-up" venture

Before you make any decisions, we recommend that you take the next quiz. While there is no surefire test, personality profile, or track record to guarantee success, collective wisdom points to key personality traits that distinguish successful entrepreneurs from those who don't make it. Defining your profile can also show you how you might partner with someone whose skills might complement yours.

Let's look at your *entrepreneurial profile.*

Circle the answer that applies best.

1. Your career has been:
    a. Primarily in small business (under 100 employees)
    b. Primarily in medium-sized business (100–500 employees)
    c. Primarily in big business (over 500 employees)

2. Did you operate any businesses before you were fifty?
    a. Many
    b. Few
    c. None

3. What is your primary motivation for starting a business?
    a. To make money
    b. So I don't have to answer to anyone else
    c. To be rich and famous
    d. As an outlet for excess energy

4. If you could choose between working hard and working smart, you would:
    a. Work hard
    b. Work smart
    c. Both

5. On whom do you rely for critical management advice?
    a. Internal management teams
    b. External management professionals
    c. External financial professionals
    d. No one except yourself

6. If you were at the racetrack, which of these would you bet on?
    a. The daily double—a chance to make a killing

b. A 10-to-1 shot

c. A 3-to-1 shot

d. The 2-to-1 favorite

7. The ingredient that is most necessary and sufficient for starting a business is:

a. Money

b. Customers

c. An idea or product

d. Motivation and hard work

8. If you were an advanced tennis player and had a chance to play a top pro like Roger Federer, what would you do?

a. Turn it down because he could easily beat you

b. Accept the challenge, but not bet any money on it

c. Bet a week's pay that you would win

d. Get odds, bet a fortune, and try for an upset

9. You tend to "fall in love" too quickly with:

a. New product ideas

b. New employees

c. New manufacturing ideas

d. New financial plans

e. All of the above

10. Which of the following personality types is best suited to be your right-hand person?

a. Creative

b. Goal-oriented

c. Fun to be with

11. You accomplish tasks better because:

a. You are always on time

b. You are organized

c. You keep good records

12. You hate to discuss:

a. Problems involving employees

b. Signing expense accounts
c. New management practices
d. The future of the business

13. If you could choose between the following professions, it would be:
    a. Professional poker player
    b. Sales
    c. Personnel counseling
    d. Teaching

14. If you had to choose between working with a partner who is a close friend or working with a stranger who is an expert in your field, you would choose:
    a. The close friend
    b. The expert

15. You enjoy being with people:
    a. When you have something meaningful to do
    b. When you can do something new and different
    c. Even when you have nothing planned

16. In business situations that demand action, clarifying who is in charge will help produce results.
    a. Agree
    b. Agree, with reservations
    c. Disagree

17. In playing a competitive game, you are concerned with:
    a. How well you play
    b. Winning or losing
    c. Both of the above
    d. None of the above

Scoring Your Entrepreneurial Profile

Now, tally your score using the chart below.

1. a = 10 b = 5 c = 0	6. a = 0 b = 2 c = 10 d = 3	11. a = 5 b = 15 c = 5	16. a = 10 b = 2 c = 0
2. a = 10 b = 7 c = 0	7. a = 0 b = 10 c = 5 d = 0	12. a = 8 b = 10 c = 0 d = 0	17. a = 8 b = 10 c = 15 d = 0
3. a = 0 b = 15 c = 0 d = 0	8. a = 0 b = 10 c = 3 d = 0	13. a = 3 b = 10 c = 0 d = 0	
4. a = 0 b = 5 c = 10	9. a = 5 b = 5 c = 5 d = 5 e = 15	14. a = 0 b = 10	
5. a = 0 b = 10 c = 0 d = 5	10. a = 2 b = 10 c = 0	15. a = 3 b = 3 c = 10	

When you add up your score, what number do you get? _____

Now, see what your score tells you about your potential success.

When compared with a group of successful entrepreneurs, your score is:

159–192	High
135–158	Comparable
114–134	Below, but still comparable
113 and under	Significantly below

Do these findings surprise you in terms of your compatibility with entrepreneurial work? If you find that you scored low, but have an excellent idea or product to take to market, you may want to look for a partner who can complement any deficiencies/weaknesses that you have. Even if your score was high, you'll still want to be sure you have a winning combination of a great product, service or idea, an opening in the market, and dependable people working with you who have complementary skills.

Margaret had done most of the legwork for her great new business idea, but knew that she needed help. Margaret was a people-person, energetic, someone who knew how to look at the big picture. She could also close a sale and was highly enthusiastic about the business mission. However, she was not very good at the operational and financial aspects of starting a business. Margaret wanted to keep her focus on marketing the company, rather than getting bogged down with the details. When she met Noreen at a luncheon, Margaret knew she had hit the jackpot. Not only was Noreen extremely organized and bright, but she had a knack for crunching numbers, managing logistics, and dealing with budgets. Noreen was the perfect complement for Margaret, and she was interested in doing something new. Together they made a great team, and the company they started is still running strong today.

Importantly, you will do well to find a first client or customer (or two) to get you going. In fact, a rule of thumb for starting a business is to have your first paying client lined up in advance. A major reason why new companies fail is that entrepreneurs spend too much time delivering the product or service they have sold and neglect marketing and sales to build the pipeline. Think of creative ways to brand yourself in the market to keep your name recognition high—and get out there and sell while delivering on your promise! Here are some ideas for sustaining brand visibility:

- Hold periodic gatherings—informal "focus groups"—to share information and gain insights on your business ideas. Find a fun place to gather colleagues, neighbors, and friends and pick their brains. They will spread the word! Holding events just to network or introduce yourself to other professionals is a great idea as well.
- Be engaged in social media. Don't just bombard audiences with one-liners and advertisements. Contribute to conversations on LinkedIn and Facebook, keep a Twitter page and share tips with your followers. Start a Facebook page for your business or start a blog and, most

importantly, ask for feedback. When customers take the time to provide feedback or comments—respond! Engagement is a powerful tool for building relationships and eventual customers.

- Stay involved! If you are not on a local or regional organization's board of directors, get on one. If you are not involved with a community group or project, get involved. If your community involvement has been centered around your children or grandchildren, make that time work for you—volunteer for events, introduce yourself to people, have fun, and get out of your office!

- Network, network, network—and make it a priority for those who work with you as well! In today's world, there is a blur between work and personal life. Take friends out to lunch, support local restaurants, stores, and organizations, be friendly to strangers, share your hobbies and interests with colleagues and at business meetings. It's all part of building relationships. People want to do business with people they trust and feel comfortable with—show your passion for your business, and it is more likely others will be intrigued and get on board.

- Write an article and submit it to your local paper or industry association journal. If you have a real story to tell, consider writing a book. A book gives you credibility and a platform to speak from. If you need help but have a great idea for a book, enlist a friend or colleague to help you write it and share credit.

- If you have a very sophisticated or complex product, consider starting an advisory committee, a group of industry specialists, clients, and business leaders who can give you ongoing advice as you grow your business. There are guidelines on how to do this, but you need to hold regular meetings and give them something back in return for their time, either a meal or a stipend.

If you still believe that you're suited to be an entrepreneur and are leaning toward giving it a try, here are some additional points for you to think about.

Twelve Steps for Entrepreneurial Success

1. *General business experience.* You'll need basic business background with the understanding of what profit and loss (P&L) statements are and "how money is made."

2. *Specific knowledge.* Be sure you have a thorough understanding of the business you're entering into. If you're buying a franchise, for example, and don't know the business, make sure you get the support and training you'll need. (Check out www.entrepreneur.com for information on franchises and other start-up advice.)

3. *Capital or clients.* Without an immediate source of revenue, your business owner status can be short-lived. Arrange a line of credit or have one or two clients lined up to start you off.

4. *Competent and trustworthy staff.* Hire people who complement the skills you don't possess—for example, if you're the marketing/sales guru, find a great finance or operations person. Get the best people you can in terms of competencies and reputation for integrity.

Gita had spent years reading, studying, and practicing yoga meditation. Her dream was to open a yoga studio when she retired. She was referred to another woman in her broad networking circle who shared her dream. Together they opened a bank account and pooled their savings in a joint checking account to draw from for the studio rental, furnishings, marketing, and advertising. Two weeks later, Gita's partner skipped town after having cleared out the account. Gita learned her lesson the hard way. Always do careful research on a person's background, reputation and trustworthiness before going into business together!

5. *Leadership skills.* As an entrepreneur, your skills as a leader and decision maker are vital to your success. You'll need to stay the course without being unduly influenced by temporary setbacks or letting others' opinions sway you.

6. *Can-do attitude.* Even when you're the head honcho, as an entrepreneur you need to substitute the big corporation attitude with "whatever it takes." As the owner of a business, you frequently need to pitch in and do the most basic tasks.

7. *Risk taking.* Going out on your own is

An important first step as you become an entrepreneur is to do a competitive analysis of the product or service you are thinking about. You may find that the space is wide open for you, in which case you can lead the way, or that the market is crowded, in which case you need to differentiate yourself.

risky and you must be willing to put your time—and perhaps money—on the line with your best effort. If you're truly afraid, or have significant ongoing financial obligations, it may not be the right step for you.

When Avery left her senior role at a consulting firm to start her own business, she had $2,500 in the bank, two children in graduate school, and was a single provider to her family. What she lacked on paper, she made up for with the absolute confidence she could be successful and woo her former clients into using her services. Risk was not an obstacle for Avery—her mind was already set, and she wasn't going to waver.

8. *Flexibility.* Market and economic conditions are ever changing, and as an entrepreneur, you have to monitor them closely and change and adapt your business strategy with them.

When the market took a downturn, Cecelia took her human resources consulting skills and applied them to outplacement counseling for her clients. When the market picked up, she went back to her executive search practice, helping her clients find top talent. Her flexibility helped her through the economic ups and downs of her business.

9. *Focus.* From the moment you start your business, be focused on the goals you have set, and keep them uppermost in your and your employees' minds at all times. If clients ask you to do something far afield from your business mission, be careful it doesn't distract you from your main focus.

10. *Sales drive.* It is your job, as business owner, to get out and sell your product or service. You are the primary spokesperson and cheerleader for your company, especially in the beginning.

11. *Juggling delivery and sales.* One of the toughest parts of starting your own business is managing your sales activity and the delivery of your product or service. The challenge is to keep an eye on both sides of your business— keep your pipeline full and the quality of your product high. No matter how interesting your current project is, you need to be out there, scouting for the next one.

12. *Independence.* As tempting as it may be in the short term, resist the urge

to bring in partners or investors in order to lighten your load. While it may help you get through a temporary crisis, it's your company; and if you give up control early on, you may be sorry.

Second/Retirement Career

Have you ever gone to work asking yourself, "What would I rather be doing right now?" Let's be honest, we've probably all asked ourselves this question at one point or another. Frequently, after devoting years of service to a particular type of work or to an organization, women feel like they need a change. When a retirement package is offered to someone who is relatively young and energetic, it may be the ideal opportunity to make the leap into a retirement or "encore" career. Or perhaps other circumstances in your life point to this type of change. If you are considering taking that leap, here are some key questions to help you think through this big decision.

- Do you have the energy to commit to a new career/new company?
- Do you want to go back to work in a full-time job?
- Are you willing to start over again, building relationships with key stakeholders and decision makers in your new company?
- Are you are thinking of launching into a new industry? Do you have the necessary skills and education?
- Do you have the contacts and financial resources to support your transition?
- If you have to step down a level in order to start over, are you okay with that?

After a decade of working for a prominent university, Addison retired as the top development officer. It was time for a new direction, and she knew she wanted to apply her skills in a different setting where she could be a more active contributor. Through her networking, she learned of a development position in a small community hospital from a friend who worked there. After her buddy paved the way, Addison obtained an interview with the HR department and eventually got the position. Not only is the hospital benefitting from having such a tenured development person on their staff, but Addison is finding enormous satisfaction in her role there. Her commitment to the goals of the hospital has given her renewed energy, and she is quickly establishing her credibility with the senior leaders in the organization and key donors in the community.

According to Encore.org—a resource for people interested in jobs that combine personal meaning, continued income, and social impact—the top five encore job fields are education, health care, environment, government, and nonprofit. While Encore.org is not a job placement service, it provides information that helps people transition to jobs in the nonprofit world and the public sector, and it might be a good place to browse. Other online sources such as AARP. org gauge some of the growing job fields, opportunities, and trends for "second act" workers and can be helpful as you explore this option.

As you network to uncover opportunities, listen carefully to how people respond to your stated retirement goal. It is possible that as well suited as you think you are for a position in a different industry or function, those who meet you may feel otherwise. If you hear resistance, probe a bit, listen to the feedback, and adjust your goals accordingly.

Consulting/Part-Time Work

Becoming a consultant/freelancer or powering down to part-time work can be a wonderful option in retirement. Some careers and skills lend themselves to this kind of working style, while others may be more difficult to fit into this mold. Or you may just want to do something entirely different—and less stressful—than the work you've done before. We've worked with a variety of executives and senior leaders who decided to go into part-time or consulting work in their retirement, and they enjoy having a more flexible schedule.

Rita was an assistant vice president for a national car rental brand she had worked with for over thirty years. Her role was invigorating and took her all over the United States to thousands of rental offices to work on their effectiveness and bottom lines. She loved her job, but the travel took up a lot of extra time and she yearned for a less hectic schedule. As a blogger for a professional organization she belonged to, she was known as an expert by people in her field. She was often approached about speaking to local groups and found she enjoyed doing the presentations. As she began to think seriously about retirement, Rita realized she could parlay her blogging and speaking into a new role as an effectiveness consultant. She felt this would not only challenge and stimulate her but also give her the flexibility she craved. She set up some meetings with her extended network and used her blog to gain exposure about her new role. When she officially retired, she already had several speaking engagements lined up around the country and, given her new flexible schedule, she used her extra time to actually explore the cities she visited.

There are many possible part-time options that may be appealing to baby boomers. Some of these, suggested by Bankrate.com, include government work, teaching/tutoring, and seasonal jobs like retail sales. Or you could consider careers that lend themselves to "virtual" part-time work. Examples of these include graphic design, market research, or programming, which can primarily be done online from a home office. Some options may require educational training or course work and, in that case, you will have to make the decision about whether this is a commitment you are willing and able to make.

Laura worked as an attorney throughout her career, and very few of her colleagues knew she had a strong artistic side. She dabbled in art projects and took some design classes, which she thoroughly enjoyed. As she approached retirement, she considered how she could apply her artistic talent to a second, part-time "career." After speaking with a friend in the advertising industry, she determined that if she took some courses to bring her design skills up-to-date with current technology, she could do freelance work for advertising agencies and business clients. She enrolled at the best local art school and prepared herself for her new freelance career.

There are a number of online resources (AARP.org, RetirementJobs.com, RetiredBrains.com) that can stimulate your thinking, and we encourage you to do a little exploring to see what possibilities are out there.

Volunteering Service Activities

Another route for those interested in part-time work would be getting involved with a community or volunteer organization. The best, most passionate, and devoted volunteers are those who feel personally invested in the success a particular organization. Our advice is to join a service or community activity with a mission or cause that you feel strongly about.

When Missy's sister was diagnosed with MS, a disease with no cure, Missy became involved in her local MS society chapter. Because she was so passionate about the cause, she became active in the chapter activities and was eventually appointed to the board. She is now able to stay on top of the latest research findings and help raise money for the cause. She feels good about the fact that she is helping her sister and many others affected by this disease.

Answer the following questions to see what cause or organization might interest you.

1. Do you have a hobby that translates into an organization or cause?
2. Do you have a friend or relative who's struggled with a physical or mental condition?
3. Is there a cultural activity which you particularly enjoy? Could this activity translate into an organization or cause?
4. Are you interested in current affairs and politics?
5. Are people you admire involved in a particular activity or organization?
6. Have you attended an organization event which you enjoyed?
7. Is there a volunteer activity or organization in which you believe you could learn and develop new skills?
8. Do you have a favorite cause to which you donate money?

Your objective is to uncover organizations that would be most rewarding for you. If your sibling is fighting an illness, that cause can be a labor of love. If you always dreamed of being a musician, joining an orchestra committee may be just right. Maybe you are crazy about your city or town since moving there two years ago—in that case, the chamber of commerce or visitors' center may be your calling.

If you're still unsure, here's another way to identify a cause that will interest you. Do any of the following categories trigger your interest? Put a check mark next to the ones you want to consider.

- Culture and the arts (orchestra, dance, museums, etc.)
- Health and humanities (United Way, American Heart Association, March of Dimes, etc.)
- Community and economic development (venture capital group, industrial development corporation, World Affairs Council, etc.)
- Local/regional business (chamber of commerce, marketing and tourism center, Rotary Club, etc.)
- Civic and public affairs (political parties and or/candidates, school boards, township associations)
- Professional and industry (American Bankers Association, American Bar Association, Human Resources Planning Society, etc.)

- Women (National Association for Female Executives, The White House Project, local women's groups)
- School alumni (college and university clubs)

Once you've narrowed down the area(s) you're interested in, you'll want to find specific local organizations that fit the bill. You can use a directory of organizations or search online (VolunteerMatch.org is a good place to start). When you find the name of an organization, ask around to see who might be familiar with it. Take a look at the current board of directors to determine if you know anyone or someone who might know someone on the board. You'll also want to go to the website and perhaps call the organization and ask them to send you any printed information they have. Chances are, when you find something specific which interests you, you'll be able to identify someone you know who is already involved or can get an introduction to someone who is. Once you express your interest in the cause, you undoubtedly will be invited to donate your time in some way.

Getting on a Board of Directors

Serving on a board of directors can be mutually beneficial to you and the organization you wish to serve. Nonprofit organizations need talented, devoted people to help champion their mission and raise awareness about their cause. A board member is a representative for the organization—and if you are committed to the cause, you will naturally be a good ambassador.

To obtain a position for a for-profit, corporate board is more difficult. You must be highly qualified and recognized for your expertise and leadership. CEOs and board-nominating committees often turn to people they know to fill board seats, so it's important to get your qualification in front of the right people. Women are often overlooked for these coveted paid positions because they are not as well-known as their male counterparts. Your best path is to start with nonprofit boards and establish yourself as a leader in that venue. Remember that you will need to contribute financially to a nonprofit board. Find out what that amount is and the meeting schedule before you pursue it further to make sure that you can fulfill the obligations of a board director.

Once you have set your sights on a particular board, here are some steps for making that goal a reality.

- Develop a board biography (see below)
- Research the current board of directors and friends of the organization
- Develop a specific networking script
- Begin networking!
- Ask for referrals

Your Board Biography

In these days of information overload, short is better, so think of your board bio as a summary of who you are and what you have to offer. Use the information in your traditional résumé to create this "executive summary" of yourself.

Advantages of the board bio are the following:

- There is no prescribed format—you are free to write it in any style or sequence.
- It contains the most favorable information about you, without the need to give a complete historical record of your employment.
- It can be scanned quickly by readers.
- It avoids the job hunter label and therefore is ideal as background information for an informational meeting.

Remember to keep your bio to about four paragraphs (one page!), and be sure the first paragraph captures the reader's attention. It's a nice touch to put a photo (a professional headshot) at the top of the page next to your name.

Biography Format

(We suggest writing in narrative style.)

Describe your work history.

_____

_____

_____

_____

Describe your major career accomplishments (quantify the results if possible).

_____

_____

_____

_____

What is your current involvement in civic, community, and volunteer opportunities?

_____

_____

_____

_____

What skills, experience, and talents can you offer to boards?

_____

_____

_____

_____

What are some of your personal hobbies and interests? A brief line about your family would also be a nice close. (Example: Mary lives in Pittsburgh, Pennsylvania, with her four children and husband.)

_____

_____

_____

_____

Sample bio

Head-shot
photo here

Bridget McMonigal

Executive Vice President,
Human Resources and Corporate Affairs
ARY Pharmaceuticals

As a member of the senior executive team of ARY Pharmaceuticals, Bridget McMonigal reports directly to the CEO of this global, $15 billion, leading biopharmaceutical company with 35,000 employees operating in over 80 countries. She is responsible for all human resources strategy, talent management, remuneration and related activities, and is accountable for internal and external communications, government affairs, corporate reputation, and corporate social responsibility. She manages a budget of $150 million and leads a team of more than 1,000 employees worldwide.

Ms. McMonigal has eighteen years of diverse experience and increasing responsibility in the pharmaceutical industry. She began her career in 1988 as an attorney in private practice in Cleveland, Ohio, focused on health care and corporate law. She joined ARY Pharmaceuticals in the legal function in 1993 and progressed to vice president of human resources for ARY's US business unit, the company's largest market. Ms. McMonigal moved to London in 2004 to lead human resources within the R&D organization, before becoming global head of corporate affairs in 2006. She was appointed to her current role in 2007.

Her strengths include strategic thinking, communication skills, ability to work globally, and leadership of diverse teams. She has significant experience in mergers and acquisitions, restructuring, downsizing, and growth. Her functional areas of expertise include legal, talent management and remuneration, communications/corporate affairs, and change management.

Ms. McMonigal received an AB, magna cum laude, from Ohio State University in 1984 and a JD from University of Connecticut School of Law in 1988. She currently resides in Wayne, Pennsylvania, with her husband and fifteen-year-old triplet daughters. In her free time, she enjoys spending time with her family, skiing, yoga, and travel.

With your bio in hand, adapt your networking script to help you as you seek board opportunities. Remember, the script should include an introduction, the purpose of the meeting (the type of board you are looking for and why), your background (skills and experiences that a board could most benefit from) and, finally, "ask" for recommendations and/or referrals. Before you leave, establish the next step.

Leisure/Family/Self-Enrichment Activities

Traditionally, retirement is thought of as a time to enjoy social and leisurely activities—and this may be *your* personal goal. Retirement is a wonderful opportunity to explore some of the activities you've never had time for.

Naomi, a former regional bank manager, worked thirty-eight years in the banking industry. In her late thirties, she took up golf, and to her surprise, she loved it. When she and her husband were two years away from retirement, they scouted out the best golfing communities in Florida. Having found their "dream home" in a beautiful development, they relocated there when they retired. Naomi is now head of the women's golf club at the country club and plays golf with her husband twice a week. Not only are they enjoying the sport and the sunshine, but they are enjoying each other's company as well. Naomi, who is a natural leader, is also using one of her major strengths as she leads the group of women.

Traveling is also a popular way to spend time in retirement. There are numerous options, including walking and biking tours, cruises, and group tours to virtually everywhere in the world. Essentially, there is something for everyone—and many special deals for baby boomers. Doing some website research here can really pay off.

For some, retirement is a time to enrich the mind or learn a new skill. Classes at colleges and universities or adult learning centers can open your mind and stimulate the brain. You may find that your appreciation of learning at this time of life is a very different experience than it was back in your college days.

Paula had a deep interest in American history but never was able to spend much time on it. A book, article, or television special from time to time had to satisfy her because of her commitments to family and job. Upon retirement, Paula applied for and was accepted to a master's program in American history at a university in her city. She is amazed at how much she enjoys the experience of academia—the courses, the people, even the experience of commuting to campus. She feels that it has opened up a new world for her and that it is keeping her mind active and stimulated.

Teaching/Coaching

Getting involved in one's community can take on many different forms. Teaching and coaching are two ways in which you might enjoy investing your time. Coaching and/or teaching are a bit different than other volunteer activities insomuch that these kinds of activities can renew an old passion for a sport or educational topic and allows a platform for sharing your knowledge with the next generation. Sometimes busy jobs take away from some of the knowledge you may be eager to share—now is your chance to make up for lost time!

Maxine landed a job at one of the big four accounting firms right out of college. She steadily worked her way up the ranks of the company, making partner in her early forties and playing a key role within the accounting firm's women's initiatives programming. As her own children graduated high school and moved out of the house, Maxine became more involved with the mentorship program at her company and very much enjoyed spending time with the young, bright female accountants just embarking on their career path. When Maxine retired in her early sixties, she wanted to continue her relationship with young people without the hours and demands of her job at an accounting firm. Maxine used her networking connections and was soon hired as an instructor at a small university near her home. This new role allowed her to share her wealth of knowledge about accounting and the industry, while also giving her a more flexible lifestyle. Maxine is now one of the most popular instructors on campus!

No matter which activity excites you, you'll need to be as fit and healthy as possible to enjoy it. Retirement also provides an opportunity to get your health, exercise regimen, and overall state of mind in good shape. The next chapter will talk about how to maintain and improve your physical, emotional, and mental well-being.

I am not young but I feel young. The day I feel old, I will go to bed and stay there. J'aime la vie! I feel that to live is a wonderful thing.
—Coco Chanel

CHAPTER 6

Maintaining Your Health in Retirement

Developing your game plan for a successful retirement is a combination of all the important issues we've discussed so far in this book. And in order to enjoy retirement and reach whatever goals you've set, it is vital to do all that you can to maintain your health. This involves taking care of yourself physically, mentally, and emotionally. You have taken a good first step by reading this book and planning your retirement goals. Why? By realistically envisioning and planning for your retirement, you will have a greater chance of being happy in the future, and studies have shown that happier people live longer, healthier lives.

As LeAnne and her husband approached their golden years, they resolved to get into better physical shape so they would be healthier and hopefully enjoy their retirement longer. They found a personal trainer who helped them work on their aerobics and conditioning, and they stayed with the program. As a result, they have newfound energy, are sleeping better, and both report feeling great.

So what can you do to be as mentally, emotionally, and physically healthy as possible in retirement?

Here are ten key tips for a healthy retirement from "Plan for Your Health," a public education campaign from Aetna and the Financial Planning Association.

1. *Know your cholesterol numbers.* A simple blood test can let you know

if you have high cholesterol. National guidelines recommend that everyone over age 20 have a blood test to determine cholesterol levels. It should include results for total cholesterol, LDL, HDL, and triglycerides. A healthy total cholesterol level is 200 mg/dL or lower. For LDL cholesterol, it is 100 mg/dL or lower. For HDL cholesterol, it is 60 mg/dL or higher. For triglycerides, it is 150 mg/dL or lower.

2. 2. *Stop smoking.* Smoking damages the heart. It raises blood pressure and damages blood vessels. It also promotes the buildup of fatty plaque in arteries and lowers levels of "good" cholesterol. This makes the blood more likely to clot and starves the heart of oxygen. Quitting smoking is the best thing you can do to help prevent a heart attack. This is easier said than done, so ask your doctor for the right kind of smoking cessation aid.

3. *Know your blood sugar numbers.* Monitor your blood sugar and maintain it at a normal level. Have a fasting blood sugar level test performed at least once a year. A normal fasting blood sugar level is less than 100 mg/dL. Higher levels indicate that you may be headed for diabetes. Risk factors for diabetes include obesity and lack of exercise. If your blood sugar level indicates a problem, work with your doctor to make changes to your lifestyle. People with diabetes are more likely to develop other health risks, such as high blood pressure and high cholesterol.

When Erin's doctor finally convinced her she needed to have her blood tested, it was discovered she had anemia. This explained a lot about the fatigue she battled and the headaches she often had. The proper medication quickly helped her, and she realized she would have to take her health more seriously from then on.

4. *Maintain a healthy weight.* Eat high-fiber foods. These include fruits, vegetables, legumes, and whole grains. You also can try oatmeal, which has a type of fiber that lowers cholesterol. Other healthy foods are brown rice, barley, peas, beans, chicken, baked fish, whole grain bread, white meat turkey, low-fat yogurt, and egg whites or egg alternatives. Avoid fad diets. They set you up to regain weight once

you resume your previous eating pattern. Most importantly, they can be dangerous because they deprive you of important nutrients.

5. *Another number to know.* Your body mass index, or BMI, relates your weight to your height. It helps to determine if you are within a healthy weight range. A BMI between 25.0 and 29.9 puts you in the overweight category. A BMI of 30.0 or higher puts you in the obese category. If you are in one of these categories, you have a greater risk of heart disease, stroke, high blood pressure, and diabetes. Check with your doctor on the right weight loss program for you if you are in one of the danger zones described above. Check out this website for more information on finding out your own BMI (http://www.cdc.gov/healthyweight/).

6. *Ease into exercise.* When starting an exercise program, be kind to your body. Don't start the first day with a thirty-minute run. Instead, start with five minutes of walking. Add one minute every day until you reach your thirty-minute-per-day goal. Talk to your doctor before you begin an exercise plan. In addition, there are now many websites and phone applications available for helping you track your exercise that make it easy to get your routine going—try the My Fitness Plan or Nike Training Club phone app or check out FitDay.com.

Tonya became increasingly unhappy and stressed about her impending retirement and decided to talk with a psychologist. Together, they uncovered that the root of her issue was her relationship with her husband and not her retirement. She and her spouse are now getting counseling and working on their marriage. The process has been one of renewal and discovery.

7. *Find a way to relax.* Too much stress can make you irritable and depressed. It also can increase your heart rate and raise your blood pressure. Relaxation eases your body's response to stress. Types of relaxation include meditation, deep breathing, muscle relaxation, listening to relaxing music, and picturing pleasant scenes. For best results, do one of these activities for fifteen to twenty minutes once or twice a day. For an easy guide

to meditation, we recommend the *Relaxation Response* by Herbert Benson.

8. *Express yourself.* Stress builds up if you keep your feelings bottled inside. Talk to your friends and family and ask for support. If you don't have a good support system, work to develop one. This way, you'll always have someone to talk to when you're upset or need advice. Women naturally form groups, confide in one another, and brainstorm solutions. Some people also keep a journal to record their thoughts and feelings. Do what works best for you.

9. *Be mindful of how you think.* Certain styles of thinking can stress you out; examples include thought processes like perfectionism, all-or-nothing thinking, and negative thinking. Be mindful of how you think. For example, if you're a perfectionist, try to lower your expectations of yourself and others, and learn to accept things you can't change. If you tend to think negatively, try to focus on the good, not the bad. Practice viewing problems as opportunities.

10. *Be aware of your blood pressure.* An optimal blood pressure level is 120/80 mmHg or less. To prevent or manage high blood pressure, consider some lifestyle changes. Cut down on salt. Limit your alcohol and caffeine intake. Quit smoking. Watch your cholesterol levels. Be physically active every day. Lose weight if you need to. Reduce stress.

Is there anything here that is a red flag for you? Perhaps you've thought about some of these issues and dismissed them because you didn't want to deal with them—or just felt like you didn't have the time. Well, now is the time!

Judy never liked going to doctors and avoided them as long as she could. She was busy 24-7 in her career and told her family she wasn't going to "look for trouble" with her health. But by the time she was approaching retirement, she knew it was time to take control by getting a comprehensive checkup. She went to her doctor and came clean about some health problems she'd been having. After diagnostic testing, several things surfaced that needed to be addressed with medication and changes in diet and exercise. Though Judy was initially upset about having to be on prescription medicine, she realized that by taking the steps her doctor recommended, she was heading off major health problems. She took her doctor's advice, made some important changes to her lifestyle, and was able to get her health on track and enjoy her retirement to the fullest.

In this book, we've talked about the financial aspects of retirement and the many changes to your routine. Even when you plan for your new situation, you may find the transition stressful. The greatest impact of retirement is often felt mentally and emotionally, especially if your sense of identity and usefulness has been tied up with your job. Keeping yourself emotionally healthy will positively impact you in many ways; you will be less prone to experience depression, and your physical health is likely to be better.

Managing Stress

Transitioning to retirement may be a time of uncertainty, but managing stress will help keep you focused on your goals. According to Bruce S. McEwan, PhD, a leading stress researcher, there are three kinds of stress.

- *Good stress* is when you are presented with a challenge, you rise to that challenge, generally have a good outcome, and you feel exhilarated. Good stress can help us learn and grow.
- *Tolerable stress* occurs when something bad happens, such as a job loss, but you have the inner resources as well as people you can turn to who help you get through it.
- *Toxic stress* is when really bad things happen and, even worse, you don't have the financial resources, internal resources, or support system to handle them appropriately. This type of stress causes emotional and physical breakdown (information from WebMD.com).

Unfortunately, it seems as if often all these different kinds of stress are in play for women and stress is at its highest in the years before retirement. Thirty percent of women in the age group 50–59 rate their stress as being from 8 to 10 on a scale of 1 to 10. Another 47 percent report a "moderate" stress level (5 to 7 on the same scale) (AARP, 2010). That same survey found that men's stress level is lower than women, particularly at the point of retirement. One can only speculate as to why, but perhaps men have been thinking and planning for retirement more strategically and much longer than women. Maybe women see their retirement years as still quite active and are more concerned about having a plan on how to continue meaningful work after

65. They may also be more concerned about earning money to sustain them and their families.

Although it's not possible to completely avoid stressful situations and thoughts, you can take steps to manage your stress and head off situations that cause it. Staying healthy, maintaining social support, keeping your spiritual life and finances in order, and developing a daily routine are all good stress-prevention tactics.

Olivia had taken a course on meditation a number of years ago, and she found that it was extremely helpful in managing her stressful life. But the demands of her schedule prevailed, and she found it more and more difficult to make the time for her meditation "practice" and eventually stopped. As she approached retirement, Olivia realized she wanted to get back to her spiritual side and vowed to make it a part of her retirement plan. After leaving her job last year, Olivia is now taking another meditation course and has incorporated yoga into her practice. She finds that these activities are helping her manage stress and maintain a positive outlook on life.

Avoiding stress in today's world is all but impossible regardless of your lifestyle or employment status. However, there are some things that can help.

- *Learn to say "no."* This can be hard for many people, but saying no to something you truly don't want to do, or don't have time for, is empowering—and can give you breathing room for other things in life.
- *Learn to let go.* Lose the self-imposed to-do list that is the root of much of our stress. Remember, the sky won't fall if you wait another day to do laundry, buy a birthday gift, or write that thank-you note.
- *Try new ways to relax.* Give some new activities a chance. Yoga and meditation work for some, while others relax through a sport like golf or walking, or activities like art, music, or reading. See what works for you.
- *Get help if you need it.* If you can't seem to get relief from your stress and nothing seems to help, talk with a doctor or counselor (information from WebMD.com).

Develop a New Routine

Though it may seem counterintuitive, the change from your hectic working schedule to a more measured pace in retirement can cause stress. Perhaps you have been so busy with work obligations that you've almost been on autopilot, going from one thing to the next. When you retire, it is important to acknowledge that many of the activities and priorities in your daily life have changed. It is equally important, for your mental and physical health, to determine what kind of schedule suits you going forward. If you decide to be laid-back and let the chips fall as they may, that may work well for you. Or you may need more structure in your life in order to feel purposeful and happy.

Clara had thought about her retirement for years and was in a good financial position when she left her company. She had been with her firm for twenty years—in fact, she'd been in the same office all that time, and her daily routine was pretty much set. So after the flurry of excitement about retiring and taking a vacation to celebrate, Clara embarked on her new life of volunteering, seeing more friends and family, and freelancing here and there. The problem was that now that she had the new, less structured retirement lifestyle she had looked forward to, she awakened each day feeling directionless. Her lack of routine was stressing her out! She realized she was a person who needed to plan her activities, so she began to create a daily/weekly routine for herself. Though very different from her old work routine, she now had a schedule and felt good about her plans for each day.

Stay Socially Connected

As you create your new routine, you'll be making decisions about whom you want to spend time with and how often. Part of your overall health is maintaining social connections with friends, family, and people with common interests. In fact, retirement may be the perfect time to reassess some of your important relationships. Now that your personal situation is changing, you may find differences in how you relate to your spouse, children, grandchildren, and good friends. For example, you may have more time to spend with family, and less contact with friends who are still working. Take the time to evaluate these situations and make adjustments to keep your relationships running smoothly.

As we grow older, particularly when we leave a corporate position, there is a danger of isolation. Building and nurturing relationships will help keep you learning and growing. You'll also maintain perspective as you gain the benefit of others' thoughts and ideas. Many women do not realize the extent of their reliance on work friendships until after retirement. There are many ways to ward off postretirement isolation, but you'll need to make more of an effort to stay in contact with people whom you no longer see regularly and who may not know your new schedule. You may also want to add new people to your life by joining a book club, gym, religious organization, or community center, depending upon your individual interests.

Alison loved to read but never had the time or the inclination to join her neighborhood book club. Many of the women who participated didn't have full-time jobs, and since Alison's job (including her commute) took up almost ten hours a day, she was happy to just "crash" when she got home and relax. After she retired, one of her acquaintances mentioned the club again, and Alison had a more positive reaction to joining. She had a great deal more free time, and she realized it might be nice to get to know her neighbors better. She also liked the idea of having a group to gather with regularly. She decided to join and found that she enjoyed the club immensely and looked forward to their monthly get-togethers.

Choose Your Exercise

Exercising is not optional! According to the Harvard School of Public Health, regular exercise keeps many of your body's systems working properly and can improve your chances of living longer. By finding exercise you enjoy, you will increase your chances of staying with it. The American College of Sports Medicine recommends moderate-intensity exercise for thirty minutes, four to five days a week, and suggests exercising with a friend or family member to help you stay on track, riding your bike or walking to complete your errands, and taking the stairs instead of the elevator as often as you can.

There are many exercise options and programs available. One of the leading exercise programs for older adults is the SilverSneakers Fitness Program, an innovative health, exercise and wellness program helping older adults live healthy, active lifestyles. This program is offered nationwide and is often a part of your local gym, YMCA, or fitness club programming. For more information, visit SilverSneakers.com.

Whatever you choose to do, it will undoubtedly be a boon to your physical as well as emotional health and well-being. If you find a friend to exercise with you, it feels a lot more social and a lot less exercise-like! So start thinking about the exercise choices that are right for you, remember not to try to do too much too soon, and get started.

Increase Your Chances for a Healthy Retirement

There are a number of things you may not be thinking about, but can do on a day-to-day basis, to boost your chances for a healthier retirement.

The following are from WebMD's "Healthy Habits to Improve Your Life."

1. *Eat breakfast every day.* Research shows people who have a morning meal tend to take in more vitamins and minerals and less fat and cholesterol.
2. *Practice good dental hygiene.* Flossing your teeth every day could add 6.4 years to your life, according to Michael Roizen, MD.
3. *Protect your skin.* Overexposure can cause sunburn, skin texture changes, dilated blood vessels, and skin cancers.
4. *Snack the healthy way.* Snacking on fruits and veggies can reduce the risk of some cancers, improve memory, and enhance your immune system.
5. *Drink water and eat dairy.* Water and milk are essential fluids for good health, but they can also help with shedding pounds.
6. *Take a daily walk.* A study of thirteen thousand people showed that people who walked thirty minutes daily had a significantly reduced chance of premature death, reports the American Council on Exercise.

Devon went to her dermatologist for her long-overdue annual visit and received a stern lecture about the condition of her skin. Her doctor pointed to her stomach where her skin was smooth and unblemished and said, "This is what your skin all over should look like!" All of a sudden, Devon's retirement dream of sunning on beaches far and wide was dashed. She realized that she would need to take care of her skin to live a long and healthy life. Melanoma is the most serious form of skin cancer and almost nine thousand people died from it in 2011. Devon decided she had better stay in the shade, so she invested in a large beach umbrella and stocked up on extra sunscreen.

Studies show that women tend to live longer than men do. If you'd like to have some fun trying to predict how long you will live, Northwestern Mutual has a game online called the "Longevity Game" that looks at your age, gender, weight/body mass, drinking/smoking habits, how you handle stress, and your driving record and then predicts your lifespan based on their actuarial expertise. To try this, you can go to media.nmfn.com. Though it's simply an estimate, you can increase your life expectancy by changing bad habits and adopting good ones. And as this test shows, the effect of our behavior is cumulative.

Jennifer Zreloff, MD, and Cynthia Barnett, EdD, put together the following checklist specifically for women over 50 (WebMD, "Women's Health") and advise that "It's a time when women need to seriously take stock of their lifestyle habits and make some changes."

So to keep mind, spirit, and health in optimal shape, here's your to-do list:

Your Checklist for Making More of Mind and Body

____*Get lots of sleep.* Maybe you got along with four hours a night when you were 40, but your body can't take that abuse when you're older. Studies show that adults over age 65 should get at least eight hours of sleep each night.

____*Set aside quiet time every morning.* Meditate, pray, visualize your day. Read something that inspires you. Focus on self-renewal.

____*Be optimistic.* Take time to understand what you want out of life. Find purpose and meaning. Then spread the joy to others.

____*Get cancer screenings.* Colon screening begins at 50. Mammograms should be annual. Pap smears continue every one to three years if you are sexually active.

___*Skin screenings.* Have an annual dermatologist check your skin all over for any signs of precancerous growths.

____*Check your bones with a bone density scan.* Talk to your doctor about calcium and vitamin D. Get at least 1,200 milligrams of calcium daily.

____*Get an annual checkup.* You need your blood pressure, cholesterol, glucose, and thyroid tested. Also, talk to your doctor about any symptoms of depression, which can be common for women over 50. These include persistent sadness or pessimism, feelings of worthlessness, loss of hope, difficulty concentrating, anxiety, and insomnia.

____*Get plenty of aerobic exercise.* It builds strong bones. It also reduces heart disease risk. Heart disease is the number one killer of women (and the number one killer of all people in 2011!).

____*Take up yoga.* Yoga is a great stretching exercise and enhances flexibility. Flexibility gives you better balance, so you don't fall—which avoids fractures.

____*Have fun.* Go bungee jumping, rock climbing, backpacking, skiing, dancing—whatever makes you happy. Act like you feel, and you'll stay youthful.

____*Eat colorful foods.* It's important for women over 50 to get plenty of fruits and vegetables. And eat more fatty fish (like salmon) to get heart-healthy omega-3 fatty acids. Learn to love whole grains, lentils, and skinless lean protein. Treat yourself to sweets but only occasionally. When you use oils, lean toward the good ones like extra-virgin olive oil.

____*Drink sensibly.* For all women, not just women over <u>50</u>, one alcoholic drink a night is plenty.

____*Find a creative outlet.* It helps prevent depression, and depression affects memory. Having a creative outlet helps stimulate your mind. Take up painting. Create a wonderful garden. Engaging your creativity stimulates your brain more than reading, and certainly more than TV.

____*Make your home an oasis.* Eliminate clutter. Fill your home with great music, books, and friends. Withdraw and recharge when you need to.

____*Associate with positive-focused people.* They will not drain your valuable energy with complaints. They will help you pursue the best that life has to offer.

Hopefully, the advice and tips on health in this chapter have motivated you to do all you can to foster that wonderful long retirement you have planned. As the authors of this checklist advise, by paying attention to these "do's," you can make *now* the best time of your life!

One day as Judy was shopping, she came upon a store in a nearby community that sold jewelry, fabrics, and pieces of sculpture. She and the shop owner began to talk and discovered they had a lot in common. In addition, the owner's partner was moving away and thinking of leaving the shop. Judy had an idea—perhaps she could buy out the partner and become a part owner. After Judy explained what she had in mind and asked some probing questions, Judy and the shop owner agreed to continue the discussion.

It took several months for Judy to consider her decision and verify that everything was in order, but eventually, she became a partner in the shop. She does the buying of the art and jewelry, contributing some of her own pieces, and her partner takes care of the fabrics. They both spend a lot of time at the store and enjoy helping their customers.

Judy never saw herself in her present role, but it has given her a new lease on life. She now tells her friends to be sure that they are doing work they enjoy. And she said, "There's no rule that says you can only have one career. I'm on my second—and who knows."

Helen

Helen was the development director for a community arts center in her town. She and her team were very successful in fund-raising and usually exceeded their goals. Through her job, she developed close friendships with hundreds of supporters and donors in the area. She always made them feel like part of a family of ardent arts lovers and community leaders, and they responded with their receptivity to the initiatives she presented.

Close to sixty-five, Helen felt young and energetic and planned on spending at least a few more years doing what she loved. However, when a new CEO came on board, Helen found him oddly disengaged and disinterested in what she did. She thought he would come around eventually, so it was a real shock when he terminated her and brought in one of his buddies to run the department. A good lawyer negotiated a generous severance package, but Helen grieved over her loss for months. Her feelings of rejection and humiliation prevented her from taking the necessary steps to pursue a new career.

Finally, she sought professional to help her move ahead with her life. When she was advised to "follow her heart," the words resonated for Helen, and she thought long and hard about what would be meaningful to her at this time of life. She had read about the fate of millions of Asian women unable to make enough money to feed their families. In many cases, they carried a stigma which ostracized them from their communities, and they often lacked any real job skills. Helen decided to enlist the help of people she knew, and she brought them together with the goal of helping struggling Cambodian women by mentoring and advising them on life and job strategies.

Helen championed the idea, gained the necessary support to move forward, and is now focused on a goal with meaning. At sixty-seven, she is planning her first trip to Cambodia to meet the women she is helping. She says that the foundational principles with which she needed to plan her future were "pleasure and purpose." In addition, she added three more Ps: *promise*—that the path on which you embark has a good likelihood of being successful, *productivity*—to be sure that what you are doing is really working and has a positive outcome, and *pizzazz*—that it is adventurous, exciting, a leap into the unknown.

Helen has found immense pleasure in her Women 4 Women group, which has really made her retirement interesting, exciting, and rewarding. She said, "Working with capable smart women has been an added bonus."

Susan

Fresh out of college and full of ambition, Susan moved from Virginia to take a job in New York City—one she describes as "the best of times, the worst of times." Over the next decades, Susan embarked on an impressive career working in human resources that eventually took her to Philadelphia and a new job opportunity.

She had been in her last job for five years when Susan was told that the company was about to be acquired. She considered this her wake-up call and decided it might be just the time to make her exit from the corporate world. Though she had made saving a priority throughout her life and was financially stable, Susan viewed retirement somewhat cautiously. She knew that she wanted to find activities that she enjoyed but was not quite sure what to do first. She decided that focusing on her health was a first step.

Since she had been a victim of severe allergies throughout her life, she started by getting help from an allergist, and to her delight, her symptoms improved dramatically. This was an important step and one she had put off for lack of time. Soon, Susan found herself feeling more energetic than she had in years, and she began exercising forty-five minutes a day.

She eventually channeled her newfound energy into horseback riding and is now very involved in the horseback riding community. One activity which Susan really enjoys is teaching children how to show and care for their horses. Susan has also joined a local organization that provides horseback riding therapy and has become active on their board. She is amazed at how many of the skills she honed during her career have served her well in her retirement.

Susan's advice to new retirees is "Don't reinvent the wheel." If there is an organization you want to be a part of or a hobby/activity that you'd like to get involved with, she advises seeking out individuals with those experiences. Susan is a great believer in "stop and smell the roses," and her days are now filled with charitable work as well as friends and relaxation. At the end of our interview, Susan made a good point, "It sounds to me a lot more like a happy non-ending!"

Liz

Liz was a senior public relations director at a local ad agency and, through her hard work and dedication, was fortunate to enjoy tremendous success. She enjoyed fun, interesting clients and thrived doing what she loved. As Liz built her client base over the years, she made important contacts across the city, and many clients became friends and trusted colleagues. As part of her job, Liz was often called upon to put together events, and her guests always gushed over how smoothly everything went and how beautiful it all looked. Liz also frequently helped her close friends plan their events but never thought about actually making it a business.

In the years leading up to Liz's retirement, she consistently sought out the advice and support of her network, including friends, colleagues, and family. When broaching the subject of retirement, she was surprised to find out how many of her colleagues suggested she start her own event business. They encouraged her to take the risk; they had faith in her and knew she could be successful at anything she put her mind to. As Liz started thinking more strategically about how she'd like to spend her days, she warmed up to the idea and began dreaming about her own event planning firm.

When the time came for Liz to retire, she was ready to take the leap. Utilizing LinkedIn, Liz created a brand for her company and began sharing insight on message boards, reaching out to old colleagues, and making new connections in her region. Liz's business has steadily grown for the last five years, and she loves her new responsibilities and clients—even though they keep her working long hours.

Liz attributes success in her retirement profession to her unwavering commitment to "delivering my best self and the best service I can provide—every day to every client." She says that even though "taking the leap is scary," if it is something you are passionate about, it is well worth the effort.

Rosa

Rosa had a wonderful thirty-five-year career as a pharmaceutical representative for a Fortune 100 company. She began her career in pharmaceutical sales right out of college where she majored in biology. She loved to sell the lifesaving drugs her company produced and felt privileged to work in an industry that was all about creating medicines to save lives. She won many awards for her achievements in sales and was promoted several times. When she reached the age and tenure that would permit her to retire with full pension and health-care benefits for life, she knew that she wanted to continue to work but decided that she wanted to make a significant life change.

Rosa's mother and aunt had both had careers as nurses, and Rosa treasured their stories about the lives they had touched. They had described the joy of helping people survive the most devastating health challenges and supporting families going through the loss of loved ones. Though Rosa held the nursing profession in the highest esteem, she had never before considered exploring nursing or medicine as a profession. Now, she felt differently—but wondered if she was too old to return to school and become a nurse.

She decided to find out and made an appointment with the dean of the nursing school nearest her home who told Rosa that her age would not be an obstacle. In fact, at fifty-six she would not be the oldest woman to enter the nursing program. She then talked with a few "mature" graduates to see how they felt about their experiences and found that all of them loved their new professions. And because there is an urgent need for skilled nurses, they had found the job market very welcoming.

Her decision made, Rosa left her company. Her nearly three years of college credits were accepted, leaving her with only a year and a half of undergraduate work to get her BS in nursing. She also decided to complete a master's in nursing, which made her an especially valuable employee. She took a position as the emergency room nurse in a local hospital and was able to match her hours to accommodate her family's schedule.

Two years later, Rosa is happy with her job, feels rejuvenated in her career, and is thankful that she took the leap into a new field. She feels that doing her research, focusing her efforts on meaningful work, and the support of her family made this change possible.

The Choice Is Yours

Each story above is unique with different twists and turns. Ultimately though, these women all shaped their retirements in ways that made them happy. What works for you is not the same kind of retirement, work, pace, or lifestyle that might work for your friend, sister, or neighbor.

By reading this book, you have begun to embrace change and growth at this pivotal prime time in your life. You are ready to embark on developing your personal road map toward a successful retirement. With each part of the process, take time to carefully consider your next steps. We hope that the book has helped you discover, or rediscover, your skills, strengths, and talents so that you can determine how to best utilize them as you craft a fulfilling retirement. Whether you choose consulting, part-time work, a new career, or more unstructured time, taking time to evaluate and strategize your retirement options will help you put together the right retirement for you. Remember, every person you meet is a potential ally in helping you reach your goals, so expanding your network is a key element in uncovering potential opportunities. And in order to enjoy your retirement, you'll need to do all that you can to maintain your health. It's this combination of factors that will lead to ultimate retirement success in which your financial, social, and lifestyle needs are met.

This is an exciting time in your life, so set yourself up for success and make the most of it! We wish you a wonderful journey!

ABOUT THE AUTHORS

 Molly D. Shepard, MS, MSM, is founder, president, and chief executive officer of The Leader's Edge/Leaders by Design, the preeminent leadership development and coaching organization dedicated to the advancement of senior executive women and men. Molly is a sought-after speaker and the author of two previous books, *Stop Whining and Start Winning* (2005) and *Breaking into the Boys' Club* (2009). Earlier in her career, Molly was chairman, president, and cofounder of Manchester Inc., one of the world's largest career development consulting firms. She is the recipient of many industry and community awards and has served on numerous public and nonprofit boards of directors. She is a trailblazer in women's leadership and a champion for women.

 **Susannah K. Cobb**, MA, a seasoned communications professional and writer, is director of client communications at The Leader's Edge/Leaders By Design, the preeminent leadership development and coaching organization dedicated to the advancement of senior executive women and men. Susannah previously worked in a marketing role for a financial services firm. She is currently pursuing her doctorate in mass media and communication at Temple University. *Preparing for Your Prime Time* is her first book collaboration.

 **Starla Crandall**, MBA, is head of research for one of the financial services programs at a large management consulting firm. She also works with a team of account executives to ensure client engagement. Starla previously worked in various marketing and development roles with the Inner-City Scholarship Fund, the American Psychological Foundation, and BoardSource. Starla received a master's in business administration from Drexel University. *Preparing for Your Prime Time* is her first book collaboration.

INDEX

CPSIA information can be obtained at www.ICGtesting.com
Printed in the USA
LVOW041409080612

285282LV00001B/4/P